D0760204

PRAISE FOR

*FAITH AND ACT: THE SURVIVAL OF MEDIEVAL
CEREMONIES IN THE LUTHERAN REFORMATION*

Ernst Walter Zeeden was one of the most important Reformation historians of the twentieth century. Years before scholars began to weigh up the vitality of late-medieval religion or trace the broad outlines of the confessionalization process, Zeeden was shedding light on a religious culture that transcended the traditional late-medieval and early modern divide while thinking of new ways to comprehend the period as a whole, an approach that eventually led to his influential idea of the "formation of confessions." *Faith and Act* was one of his earliest and most important works in this vein, a mix of exacting research and historiographical vision that may justly be viewed as one of the foundation texts of modern Reformation history.

—C. Scott Dixon, PhD
Queen's University, Belfast

For 50 years Zeeden's work has shaped historians' knowledge of the confessionalizing of religious life and practice in Reformation-era Europe. *Faith and Act* provides a masterful account of the ritual system of the churches in Protestant Germany by means of a close analysis of the documents through which the Reformers both preserved and adapted elements of the Catholic tradition. Historians of liturgy and church discipline will welcome the re-appearance of Zeeden's classic monograph, gracefully translated and with updated bibliographical references.

—Ralph Keen, PhD
Professor of History
Arthur J. Schmitt Foundation Chair in Catholic Studies
University of Illinois at Chicago

Kevin Walker's translation of *Faith and Act* represents a necessary addition to contemporary scholarship on how liturgical practices shaped the lived religion of the Reformation churches. Zeeden's original book was visionary in many ways; it anticipated both the scholarly discussion over confessionalization that has dominated the last generation of Reformation scholarship and the debate inspired by Gerald Strauss over the relative success or failure of the Reformation. Walker's translation brings Zeeden's original insights to light for an Anglophone audience, and his preface and notes update the scholarly apparatus to account for over fifty years of scholarship inspired by, and in dialogue with, Zeeden's original. Walker's additions never overshadow the text, however, and his explanation of ecclesiastical terminology in the preface provides a remarkably clear window into the diverse and potentially overwhelming world of organizational, disciplinary, and liturgical practices that characterized the nascent Lutheran churches. Taken as a whole, this new translation of Zeeden's *Faith and Act* reveals a fluid religious culture in which secular and ecclesiastical leaders strove to synthesize traditional forms of worship with novel theological insights; this depiction adds depth and specificity to our knowledge of that process of synthesis, and delightfully unsettles easy generalizations about the transition from medieval to early modern Christianity.

—Phillip Haberkern, PhD
Assistant Professor of History
Boston University

Ernst Walter Zeeden's *Katholische Überlieferungen in den lutherischen Kirchenordnungen des 16. Jahrhunderts* is one of the most important works of German research from the past half century concerning the history of the Reformation and its ramifications. For comparative historical research of confessions, which consequently became focused under the key concepts of "confessional formation" and "confessionalization," this book represented a decisive breakthrough in terms of methodology and substance. Zeeden was able to show that the separation of the confessions in the everyday religious life of people in the Holy Roman Empire was a slow process that stretched over several generations. In doing so, he qualified firmly ingrained views of history of Protestant and Catholic historians (and theologians), who had presumed an early separation of the confessions: Some saw the "introduction of the Reformation" at the earliest possible fixed date (with the first evangelical sermon and celebration of the Lord's Supper under both kinds), others in the successful defense of Catholicism and beginning of the Counter-Reformation, also preferably as early as the 1520s and 1530s (with territorial prohibition mandates). By way of contrast, Zeeden pointed to the numerous cases of interference and mixed forms in practice, in which the old Church and new faith coexisted in many German territories and cities. Closed confessional states among the territories of the Empire were for a considerable time more the exception than the rule. The dogmatic confessional definitions of doctrine (Augsburg Confession, Council of Trent, Heidelberg Catechism) were put into practice in worship, piety, and everyday life also very gradually at first and with numerous compromises. In conjunction with this, Zeeden also drew attention to the significance of cultural-historical phenomena (art, literature, popular customs). It is to be highly welcomed that now after half a century this groundbreaking study for research is being translated into English.

—Professor Dr. Anton Schindling
Fachbereich Geschichtswissenschaft
Seminar für Neuere Geschichte
Philosophische Fakultät
Eberhard-Karls-Universität Tübingen

This book would be a helpful contribution to Lutheran theology and church life if it offered only an English translation of Zeeden's classic study, which made clear the dense catholicity of earliest Lutheran church practice. Translator Kevin G. Walker offers here much more. In a highly informative preface, as well as dozens of new footnotes, he breathes new life into the work, making it much more useful and relevant for today. For everyone who really cares how the Lutheran Reformation came to life in a rich but varied liturgical practice, this book, now more than ever, is essential reading.

—Mickey Mattox, PhD
Associate Professor of Theology
Director of Undergraduate Studies in Theology
Marquette University

Kevin Walker has done us a service through his translation of Ernst Zeeden's monumental study of the Lutheran church orders of the sixteenth century. These documents provide a unique insight into the Lutheran Reformation, both the successes it enjoyed as well as the perennial challenges and occasional failures. Anyone interested in the development of Lutheran liturgical practice, especially in light of medieval milieu from whence it came, will find *Faith and Act* to be an engaging resource.

—Paul Grime, PhD
Associate Professor of Pastoral Ministry and Missions
Concordia Theological Seminary, Fort Wayne, IN

A gripping read awaits those who attend to Zeeden's multi-faceted account of the nitty-gritty of classical Lutheran church life in its parish and public setting. As he shows how the first generations committed to the Augustana took care not to throw out the 'catholic' baby with the tainted 'medieval' water, a master historian of another confession poses searching questions to

Lutherans of the present day. I commend Kevin Walker for toiling to make this significant study available to the reading public of the Anglosphere.

—John R Stephenson, PhD
Professor of Historical Theology
Concordia Lutheran Theological Seminary, St. Catharines, Ontario

This meticulous historical study examines the complexities of liturgical practices in sixteenth century Lutheranism as reflected in the church orders. *Faith and Act: The Survival of Medieval Ceremonies in the Lutheran Reformation* is an invaluable handbook providing detailed and documented data giving contemporary readers a glimpse into the way that liturgical texts and ceremonies were retained, modified, or rejected in various territories. Liturgical scholars as well as pastors will find this volume to be a useful guide to understanding the evangelical reception and appropriation of the catholic legacy of liturgical forms and practices in light of the immediate background of the medieval church.

—John T. Pless, MDiv
Assistant Professor of Pastoral Ministry and Missions
Director of Field Education
Concordia Theological Seminary, Fort Wayne, IN

What a service Kevin G. Walker has done for the Lutheran Church in English speaking lands by providing this fine translation of Ernst Zeeden's helpful monograph: *Faith and Act: The Survival of Medieval Ceremonies in the Lutheran Reformation*. Both the medieval practices and the details of the early Lutheran appropriation of them are not nearly as well known as they ought to be, and this volume goes a long way towards remedying that. I heartily recommend the book to any and all who love the Lutheran liturgy and seek to become better acquainted with its formative development in the time of the great Church Orders. It's the next best thing to having a full set of Sehling gracing your shelf!

—William C. Weedon, STM
Director of Worship
The Lutheran Church Missouri Synod

FAITH AND ACT

FAITH AND ACT

THE SURVIVAL OF MEDIEVAL CEREMONIES
IN THE LUTHERAN REFORMATION

ERNST WALTER ZEEDEN

TRANSLATED BY

KEVIN G. WALKER

Peer Reviewed

CONCORDIA PUBLISHING HOUSE · SAINT LOUIS

Concordia
Publishing House

Peer Reviewed

Published 2012 by Concordia Publishing House

3558 S. Jefferson Ave., St. Louis, MO 63118–3968

1-800-325-3040 · www.cph.org

English translation copyright © 2012 Kevin G. Walker

All rights reserved. No part of this publication may be reproduced, stored in a retrieval system, or transmitted, in any form or by any means, electronic, mechanical, photocopying, recording, or otherwise, without the prior written permission of Concordia Publishing House.

Originally published as *Katholische Überlieferungen in den lutherischen Kirchenordnungen des 16. Jahrhunderts.* [Catholic Traditions in Lutheran Church Orders of the Sixteenth Century] © copyright 1959 by Aschendorff in Münster, Germany

Cover: Courtesy of the Digital Image Archive, Pitts Theology Library, Candler School of Theology, Emory University.

Manufactured in the United States of America

Library of Congress Cataloging-in-Publication Data

Zeeden, Ernst Walter.

[Katholische Überlieferungen in den lutherischen Kirchenordnungen des 16. Jahrhunderts. English]

Faith and act : the survival of medieval ceremonies in the Lutheran Reformation / Ernst Walter Zeeden ; translated by Kevin G. Walker.

p. cm.

Includes indexes.

ISBN 978-0-7586-2701-8

1. Lutheran Church--Liturgy--History--16th century. 2. Lutheran Church--History--16th century. 3. Catholic Church--Liturgy--History--16th century. 4. Catholic Church--History--16th century. I. Title.

BX8067.A1Z4413 2012

264'.04109031--dc23   2012003084

This material is being released for study and discussion purposes, and the author is solely responsible for its contents. It has not been submitted to the process for doctrinal review stipulated in the Bylaws of The Lutheran Church—Missouri Synod and does not necessarily reflect the theology of the Lutheran Confessions or the doctrinal position of The Lutheran Church—Missouri Synod.

1 2 3 4 5 6 7 8 9 10   21 20 19 18 17 16 15 14 13 12

TABLE OF CONTENTS

CONCORDIA UNIVERSITY LIBRARY
PORTLAND, OR 97211

TRANSLATOR'S PREFACE

Major developments changed the scene of the sacred and the secular as the late Middle Ages yielded to the early modern era. Lutheran reforms had far-reaching effects, both direct and indirect. One might be surprised, however, to learn of things that did not change with the Reformation, or at least not right away. The work presented here by E. W. Zeeden shows us clearly that the Reformation did not happen overnight—neither with the posting of the Ninety-Five Theses, nor with the presentation of the Augsburg Confession. Although he does express his own opinions and conjectures along the way, the Roman Catholic Zeeden avoids polemics, seeking rather to be a faithful historian who presents the facts and lets them speak for themselves. Of the numerous works he has written dealing with the Reformation and the Counter-Reformation, one volume has previously been made available in English: *The Legacy of Luther: Martin Luther and the Reformation in the Estimation of the German Lutherans from Luther's Death to the Beginning of the Age of Goethe*, translated by Ruth Mary Bethell (Westminster, Md.: Newman Press, 1954). The work before you focuses on Lutheran church orders of the sixteenth century and provides an intriguing display of the complex interaction between personal faith and habit, the way people worship and the way they believe, the ruler's right to determine the religion of his land and the religion actually adhered to by the people,[1] as well as the impact that economic conditions and the governing forms of church and state had on the life of the church. While the author of such a work may be judged by what he has or has not included, it must be remembered that Zeeden makes no claim to completeness, but rather refers to this as an exploratory overview. It is an invitation to get acquainted with the source documents and explore them more widely and deeply than others have done before.[2]

---

[1] These two laws are sometimes referred to as *lex orandi est lex credendi et agendi* (the rule of prayer is the rule of creed and deed) and *cuius regio, eius religio* (whose the region, his the religion).

[2] Some church order excerpts have been translated into English and form Chapter 3 of *Documents from the History of Lutheranism, 1517–1750*, ed. by Eric Lund (Minneapolis: Fortress Press, 2002); for orders by Johannes Brenz

Originally published in 1959, this book followed an article employing a term that was to become groundbreaking in the study of early modern Church History: *Konfessionsbildung* (formation of confessions, confessional formation, or confession-building).[3] As stated by Anton Schindling, "His approach overcame older confessionalistic models of interpretation in historiography that either understood Protestantism as a dynamic one-way street into the

---

in particular, see *Godly Magistrates and Church Order: Johannes Brenz and the Establishment of the Lutheran Territorial Church in Germany 1524–1559* by James M. Estes (Toronto: Centre for Reformation and Renaissance Studies, 2001). As an example of more recent German research into church orders, one may look to the collection of essays entitled *Gesammelte Aufsätze: zu den Kirchenordnungen des 16. Jahrhunderts*, ed. by Anneliese Sprengler-Ruppenthal (Tübingen: Mohr Siebeck, 2004).

Studies in English providing more insight into the rites, worship, and church polity of the period include *Johannes Brenz and the Problem of Church Order in the German Reformation* by James Martin Estes (Ph.D. diss., Ohio State University, 1964), *An Historical Survey of the Liturgical Forms in the Church Orders of Johannes Bugenhagen (1485–1558)* by Loui Novak (Th.D. diss., Iliff School of Theology, 1974), *"Ordo et Libertas": Church Discipline and the Makers of Church Order in Sixteenth-Century North Germany* by Jeffrey Philip Jaynes (Ph.D. diss., Ohio State University, 1993), *Pastors and Parishioners in Württemberg During the Late Reformation, 1581–1621* by Bruce Tolley (Stanford: Stanford University Press, 1995), *The Reformation and Rural Society: The Parishes of Brandenburg-Ansbach-Kulmbach, 1528–1603* by C. Scott Dixon (Cambridge: Cambridge University Press, 1996), *The Reformation of Ritual: An Interpretation of Early Modern Germany* by Susan C. Karant-Nunn (London; New York: Routledge, 1997), *Worship Wars in Early Lutheranism: Choir, Congregation, and Three Centuries of Conflict* by Joseph Herl (New York; Oxford: Oxford University Press, 2004), and *Christian Magistrate and Territorial Church: Johannes Brenz and the German Reformation* by James M. Estes (Toronto: Centre for Reformation and Renaissance Studies, 2007).

[3] Ernst Walter Zeeden, "Grundlagen und Wege der Konfessionsbildung in Deutschland im Zeitalter der Glaubenskämpfe," *Historische Zeitschrift* 185 (1958): 249–299. Zeeden expanded on this work in a book published seven years later: *Die Entstehung der Konfessionen: Grundlagen und Formen der Konfessionsbildung im Zeitalter der Glaubenskämpfe*. München; Wien: Oldenbourg, 1965. Later he republished articles from books and journals as a collection: *Konfessionsbildung: Studien zur Reformation, Gegenreformation und katholischen Reform*. Stuttgart: Klett-Cotta, 1985.

modern world or Catholicism as the ever-constant, steadfast old Church."[4] Zeeden, who passed away this year, has been hailed as a pioneer, whose approach to research paved the way for the concept now commonly referred to as confessionalization.[5] While this concept has received a fair amount of treatment, largely due to the work of Wolfgang Reinhard and Heinz Schilling,[6] study devoted to the church orders and visitation records is still underrepresented. That being the case, the work before you remains a valuable contribution to our understanding of how the Lutheran confession took shape, as it draws from numerous primary sources little tapped elsewhere.

To increase the book's usefulness I have added numerous references and explanations. As a way of helping the reader understand the historical setting, at this point we turn to a brief discussion of terminology relating to the ecclesiastical offices encountered in this book. For us the word "pastor" (Latin for

---

[4] "Maßgeblich an der Etablierung des Fachteilgebiets 'Geschichte der Frühen Neuzeit' beteiligt: Zum Tode von Professor Dr. Ernst Walter Zeeden ein Nachruf von Anton Schindling" in the *Leute* section of the newsletter *Uni Tübingen aktuell* No. 4/2011.

[5] In an essay entitled "Delayed Confessionalization: Retarding Factors and Religious Minorities in the Territories of the Holy Roman Empire, 1555–1648," Anton Schindling differentiates the concepts: "The term *Konfessionsbildung* emphasizes the process of spiritual and theological discussion and definition within the church that resulted in the formulation of a binding confession.... By contrast, the more comprehensive term *Konfessionalisierung* embraces the implications for state, politics, society, and culture that resulted from the definition of the confession" (p. 54 in *State and Society in Early Modern Austria*, ed. by Charles W. Ingrao, West Lafayette, Ind.: Purdue University Press, 1994).

[6] For an explanation and critique of the approach of Reinhard and Schilling, see "The Concept of 'Confessionalization': a Historiographical Paradigm in Dispute" by Ute Lotz-Heumann, *Memoria y Civilización* 4 (2001): 93–114, and more recently "Confessionalization and Literature in the Empire, 1555–1700" by Ute Lotz-Heumann and Matthias Pohlig, *Central European History* 40 (2007): 35–61. See also *Confessionalization in Europe, 1555–1700: Essays in Honor and Memory of Bodo Nischan*, ed. by John M. Headley, Hans Joachim Hillerbrand, and Anthony J. Papalas (Aldershot, Hants; Burlington, Vt.: Ashgate, 2004). For a study of confessionalization that narrows its scope to the exclusion of Roman Catholicism, see *Lutherans and Calvinists in the Age of Confessionalism* by Bodo Nischan (Aldershot, Hampshire; Brookfield, Vt.: Ashgate/Variorum, 1999).

"shepherd") generally denotes any ordained minister. In German, however, "*Pastor*" was not always used generally. For any ordained minister a common word is "*Geistlicher*," which is translated here as "clergyman"; another is "*Seelsorger*" (curate), one who is responsible for *Seelsorge/cura animarum* (care of souls); "*Priester*" (priest) also continued to be used for this purpose in Lutheran churches, whereas "*Pfaffe*" took on a pejorative connotation. Another common word in German, today generally used as we use "pastor," is "*Pfarrer*." Also in the sixteenth century, *Pfarrer* is used synonymously with *Pastor*, but one should not automatically assume with this that any ordained minister is meant. Only a *Pfarrer* in the sense of the old polity could be called *Pastor*.[7] Since modern usage of "pastor" deviates from the old sense, the following should help the reader better understand the hierarchical system that was in place and why "*Pfarrer*" is not simply rendered as "pastor" in this translation.

Regions were divided into parishes,[8] and a parish (*Pfarrei*) would generally have at least one church and one pastor called *Pfarrer* or *Pfarrherr*, literally "lord of the parish." English has a word from medieval Latin meaning the same thing, namely, "parson."[9] Parishes

---

[7] Sehling (5:20) expressly states that this was the case in Dorpat (a city in northeastern Livonia, now Tartu, Estonia). In general, the terms appear to be used interchangeably throughout the church orders; also in the Lutheran Confessions, the Latin equivalent for *Pfarrer* is usually either *pastor* or *parochus*. Zeeden himself sometimes writes *Pastor* when *Pfarrer* is the word used by his source. Although distinctions may appear to be made at times, I have not found any true distinction in the church orders. For example, the 1570 church order for Kurland (now part of Latvia) lists: "*pastores, pfarhern, diaconi, seelsorger und kirchendiener*" (Sehling 5:80), but an earlier listing and discussion (58f.) shows that *Pfarrer* and *Pastor* are synonymous. In another place, the great church order of 1580 from Elector August of Saxony, it might seem that the distinction between *Pfarrer* and *Pastor* is that of serving in a city or village, respectively (Sehling 1:384); later however, in the "Visitation and Superintendence Order" portion, it is clear that *Pfarrer* also refers to village clergy (393f.).

[8] A parish could also be limited to personal property (for example, a nobleman's court) or that of an institution.

[9] We have another word from Latin, "rector" (ruler), which is also used as a title for a *Pfarrer*, as well as for the leader of an academic institution. Although Anglicans and Scandinavian Lutherans use this term to refer to a *Pfarrer*, it is not common among German or American Lutherans, nor have I found it used this way in the church orders. Sehling does not index the term,

that did not have their own parson, and possibly lacked their own church building, were affiliated with a mother parish and called out-parishes (*Filiale*). As "lord of the parish," the parson would live in the parsonage (*Pfarrhaus*), take possession of parish land called glebes (*Pfarräcker*), and possibly receive benefices, prebends, and tithes.[10] He would be the "head pastor" of the parish, thus he would be responsible for the pastoral care of all his parishioners (*Pfarrkinder*) and all other clergy serving his parish would be subordinate to him and bear a different title: preacher (*Prediger/Predikant*), deacon (*Diakon*), and chaplain (*Kaplan/Capellan*),[11] for example. These

---

but I have found *rector*, *conrector*, and *subrector* used to denote school leaders (for example Sehling 3:146, 278, 293; 5:301–2, 495–7, 555).

[10] Parishioners tithed their food and animals to support church workers in addition to putting alms in the offering box and paying occasional fees (see the note on small tithes in Part 2 of Chapter 2). Prebends and benefices are explained in the first footnote of Chapter 2.

[11] The terms for "chaplain" and "deacon" are sometimes used synonymously. Even as *Seelsorger* (curate) typically refers to a clergyman in general, but sometimes to an assistant pastor in particular, so also *Prediger* (preacher). Any clergyman could be called a preacher, since all are ordained to the *Predigtamt* (preaching office), but some were called specifically to fill a preaching benefice, in which they may have been free of other pastoral responsibilities. Already in the fifteenth century, "the laity came increasingly to consider itself responsible for the church's constitution and performance. This was an impulse which had long been at work, principally in the cities. Territorial princes and city magistrates, even individual citizens, took energetic action in matters of monastic reform, and toward the turn of the century it became customary to endow preaching benefices for the purpose of guaranteeing regular sermons of high quality (as is proved by the frequent stipulation that incumbents should hold a university degree), as a result of which many regions, especially in southwest Germany, had at least one endowed preacher in almost every city" (p. 194 in "Religious Life in Germany on the Eve of the Reformation" by Bernd Moeller, pp. 189–198 in *Contesting Christendom: Readings in Medieval Religion and Culture*, ed. by James L. Halverson, Lanham: Rowman & Littlefield, 2008, first published in *Pre-Reformation Germany*, ed. by Gerald Strauss, London: Macmillan, 1972. Reproduced with permission of Palgrave Macmillan.). Andreas Wagner wrote similarly about this, noting that the preachers who received these preaching benefices had to have a theological education, and that it was not rare for this education to surpass that of the local parson (cf. p. 72 of Wagner's doctoral thesis, *Das Falsche der Religionen bei Sebastian Franck*, Berlin 2007). "The special tasks of these preachers was usually to instruct

ministers were basically "assistant pastors." (Note: There was also a diaconal office in which laity had charge over funds and food in the common chest.) The term vicar (*Vikar/Vicarius*) had various usages: a clergyman ministering in the stead of a parson (like a vacancy pastor), an assistant minister, or a young theologian assigned to assist and receive training from a parson. Numerous church orders say that they are to help parsons, preachers, and chaplains with hearing confession and administering the Sacrament; they are also regularly to help sing the daily offices, receive the Sacrament, and listen to sermons.[12] All of the above could be called ministers of the church or church workers (*ministri ecclesiae/Kirchendiener*) in the narrow sense, while others under the parson's authority could also be called this in the wide sense: sacristan/sexton (*Küster/Mesner/Kirchner*),[13] bell-ringer (*Glöckner*), schoolmaster (*Schulmeister*), teaching assistant (*Schulgeselle*), cantor, and organist.[14] In addition to preparing the altar and baptismal font and maintaining the church grounds, the duties of the sacristan usually included bell-ringing (thus *Glöckner* was frequently used in the wide sense to denote a sacristan), but could also include working the organ bellows (otherwise done by *calcanten*,

---

the townspeople from the Bible and the Church Fathers as well as to catechize the youth" (p. 25 of Peter Blickle, *Die Reformation im Reich*, 3rd ed., Stuttgart: E. Ulmer, 2000, quoted by Wagner).

[12] Cf. Sehling 3, passim. A vicarage (*Vikarei*) was an office or position bound with a certain income; in this way, other church workers could also be called vicars. Thus in the 1578 visitation decree for Stendal, for example, the organist and choirmaster are called vicars (Sehling 3:318).

[13] The terms "sacristan" and "sexton" are used synonymously, even as the three German terms are used interchangeably (see the *DWB* entries for "Küster," "Meszner," and "Kirchner," which are all defined by the Latin "*aedituus*" and a term for "bell-ringer" as well as other related terms). Since the office usually included many more responsibilities (cf. note 15) than what is currently understood today by the words "sacristan" and "sexton," the term "clerk" is sometimes used, as in *Worship Wars in Early Lutheranism: Choir, Congregation, and Three Centuries of Conflict* by Joseph Herl (New York; Oxford: Oxford University Press, 2004); I have chosen to retain "sacristan" and "sexton" since I use "clerk" for "*Schreiber*."

[14] A teacher bearing the title *baccalaureus* or *infimus* had not attained the rank of master, thus was a teaching assistant or intern. Cantors and organists were also counted as teaching assistants. *Schulmeister* and *Schulgesellen* were also called *Schuldiener*, school ministers or workers.

bellows-treaders), as well as catechizing, teaching, preaching, and visiting the sick.[15]

Moving in the other direction of the hierarchy, a parson could be made a superintendent (*Superintendent/Superattendent*)[16] or bishop[17] to oversee other parsons and church workers; carrying out this office involved church and school visitations.[18] Above these would be a general superintendent or archbishop. With the intermingling of church and state it also happened that a prince's authority extended so far over the church that he took the title of chief bishop (*summus episcopus*). Beyond this there were also consistories[19] and synods,[20]

---

[15] For a list of the sacristan's duties as described in the 1581 church order for Hoya, see Herl, 42; see also an excerpt from the 1528 church order for Braunschweig and from the "General Articles" from 1557 for the visitation in Electoral Saxony (Lund, 148f., no. 85; for the full and lengthy description in the latter, see Sehling 1:326–8).

[16] See, for example, the corresponding section in Melanchthon's 1528 "Instructions for the Visitors of Parish Pastors in Electoral Saxony" (*LW* 40, 313f.) and the "General Articles" from 1557 for the visitation in Electoral Saxony (Sehling 1:320f.). No one was to be made superintendent without the elector's approval (Sehling 1:334).

[17] Although largely replaced by the term "superintendent," the term "bishop" was still used among Lutherans for this office. Examples include Nicholas von Amsdorf, Georg von Polentz, Erhard von Queiß, Paul Speratus, Eberhard von Holle, and Johannes Wigand, not to mention bishops in Scandinavia, where there was also an archbishop, Laurentius Petri.

[18] See Sehling 1:69ff. for a discussion of various types of visitations (general, special, local, and particular). The 1577 visitation instruction for Saxony says that the superintendents and their adjuncts are to visit each parish and church assigned to them within their district at least twice a year (Sehling 1:348); however, finding the money required to travel around was problematic, and the time demands on the superintendents prevented them from fulfilling their other duties (Sehling 1:72f.). For an example of what a visitation entails, see the visitation instructions in the 1537 church order for Hesse (Lund, 147f., no. 84) or the instructions mentioned above in note 16. Synods could also be referred to as visitations when, instead of the visitors traveling to various parishes, the people to be visited traveled to the visitors (Sehling 1:69).

[19] An example of the makeup of a consistory can be seen in the consistorial order of 1584 issued by Margrave Georg Friedrich of Ansbach as Regent of Prussia; it specified that the consistory should be composed of *ecclesiasticae* and *politicae*, in particular, a court counselor, two lawyers, the general superintendent, the primary professor of Theology at the university, and a

both of which were generally made up of clergy and laity. This is the basic structure, but does not exhaust the list of positions and designations (much less spelling variations!) encountered in the church orders.

---

pastor (Sehling 4:123). Werner Elert says that according to Melanchthon's 1545 "Wittenberg Reformation," the government should establish ecclesiastical courts, which are consistories. "They are by no means mere administrative organs. On the contrary, they are also criminal courts in the strict sense of the term. Their judgment, it is true, 'does not put man to death with the sword; but it punishes with the Word of God and with separation or ejection from the church.' Thus when the key of binding is used, they support the pastor on the basis of the judgment of the church as a whole. . . . But even when the powers are delimited, there arises a point of view that cannot be derived from the Office of the Keys itself. This ecclesiastical court is competent as a penal court in cases 'which the secular government does not want to consider' " (p. 381 in *The Structure of Lutheranism*, trans. by Walter A. Hansen, St. Louis: Concordia Publishing House, 1962, Melanchthon's text in *CR* 5, 604). Lund says there were three consistories in Electoral Saxony and provides an excerpt from the Wittenberg consistorial order of 1542 concerning cases to be heard by the consistory (Lund, 149f., no. 86). According to the "General Articles" from 1557 for the visitation in Electoral Saxony, no city or village parson was to be accepted without the foreknowledge of the consistory and the local superintendent (Sehling 1:334). See also the "Consistory, consistorial organization" article by Sehling in *The New Schaff-Herzog Encyclopedia of Religious Knowledge*, vol. 3, p. 246f. (ed. by Samuel M. Jackson, Grand Rapids: Baker Book House, 1952).

[20] The term "synod" could be used as a synonym of "visitation" (called a special or particular synod) or to designate a body that gave counsel or decided on actions to take (a general synod, Sehling 1:71f.). In Saxony, Elector August instituted the general synod, which consisted of theologians and counselors and met twice a year with the superintendents to discuss the visitation records and decide on how to address whatever shortcomings or offenses had been identified (Sehling 1:73). Also worthy of note is James M. Estes' discussion of the consistorial system and synods in Württemberg (pp. 20–30 of *Godly Magistrates and Church Order: Johannes Brenz and the Establishment of the Lutheran Territorial Church in Germany 1524–1559*, Toronto: Centre for Reformation and Renaissance Studies, 2001). There, "synod" referred to the consistory enlarged by general superintendents; the synod discussed the findings of visitations and recommended actions to be taken by the duke based on this. It also had the right to excommunicate, instead of leaving this up to individual pastors.

Though rarely encountered in Lutheran churches, cathedral and collegiate church chapters are another aspect of the church organization. A chapter is a body of canons (clergy) headed by a dean and/or provost and associated with a particular cathedral or collegiate church where they were responsible for conducting or singing services.[21] In contrast to collegiate churches, cathedrals were served by bishops. "After the Reformation the chapters which came over to the new doctrine with their bishops were usually dissolved; but a few of them succeeded in maintaining their existence in spite of the local sovereign, especially those which did not become wholly Protestant and went on as 'mixed chapters' (Osnabrück, Halberstadt, Minden), with a system of alternation as to the bishopric between the two religions, lasting even through the Peace of Westphalia [1648]. The connection of the others with the bishops who had become Protestants did not last long, and most of them were sooner or later incorporated with the territories of the sovereigns who had at first been their administrators."[22]

Concerning names of people and places, note that we have kept the German forms for German people and cities (thus Friedrich instead of Frederick, Georg : George, Heinrich : Henry, Johann and Johannes : John,   Wilhelm : William,   Nürnberg : Nuremberg, Braunschweig : Brunswick), except for Smalcald and some cities added to the map for reference. Instead of Courland, we have kept Kurland; instead of March : Mark (a borderland), although compounds have been partially anglicized (thus Old Mark for Altmark, New Mark : Neumark, Electoral Mark : Kurmark). All other lands and regions have been anglicized. For those interested in knowing the German behind the English terms for rulers and their lands encountered in this study, here is an overview in ascending rank:[23]

---

[21] Canons were generally supported by receiving a canonry, that is, a prebend or benefice, and had a vote in the chapter.
[22] "Chapter" by Albert Hauck in *The New Schaff-Herzog Encyclopedia of Religious Knowledge*, vol. 3, p. 9 (ed. by Samuel M. Jackson, Grand Rapids: Baker Book House, 1952).
[23] The middle of this hierarchy is approximate, due to the emperor's ability to grant or deny privileges and the ability of some rulers to acquire greater power, often the result of infighting amongst the nobility. See *The Feud in Early Modern Germany* by Hillay Zmora (Cambridge; New York: Cambridge University Press, 2011). For a good exposition of how these

baron / barony	*Freiherr / Standesherrschaft*
count / county	*Graf / Grafschaft*
prince / principality	*Fürst / Fürstentum*
landgrave / landgraviate	*Landgraf / Landgrafschaft*
margrave / margraviate	*Markgraf / Markgrafschaft*
count palatine / palatinate	*Pfalzgraf / Pfalzgrafschaft*
duke / duchy	*Herzog / Herzogtum*
(prince-)elector / electorate	*Kurfürst / Kurfürstentum*

All together there were seven electors, who had the right to elect the emperor of the Holy Roman Empire: the Duke of Saxony, the Margrave of Brandenburg, the Count Palatine of the Rhine, the King of Bohemia, and the archbishops of Mainz, Trier, and Köln (Cologne). Next to the emperor, the most powerful rulers were the electors. It should be noted that "prince" (*Fürst*) was used not only as a specific title, but also as a general title referring to any ruler ranking above him on this list, including the elector; they all classify as high nobility. Likewise, "principality" could refer to the land of any of these princes.

The border history of the various lands and territories in and around the Holy Roman Empire involves frequent fluctuation due to distribution among heirs, battles, and annexation, but in an attempt to help the reader visualize the abundant geographical references, we have added to Zeeden's text a map showing the approximate boundaries during the sixteenth century. If greater detail is desired, one may consult an historical atlas, such as Earle W. Dow's *Atlas of European History* (New York: Henry Holt, 1909). Our map is largely based on Plate 18 of this work. A good German counterpart is Map 7 of the *Kleiner Atlas zur deutschen Territorialgeschichte*, Bernhart Jähnig and Ludwig Biewer (Bonn: Kulturstiftung der Deutschen

---

various rulers and lands related to one another in the fourteenth century and earlier, see *Princes and Territories in Medieval Germany* by Benjamin Arnold (Cambridge; New York: Cambridge University Press, 1991). Also of interest here is *Reformation and the German Territorial State: Upper Franconia, 1300–1630* by William Bradford Smith (Rochester: University of Rochester Press, 2008) and *Nobilities in Transition, 1550–1700: Courtiers and Rebels in Britain and Europe* by Ronald G. Asch (London: Arnold Publishers, 2003).

Vertriebenen, 1989). For more details concerning lands east of the Holy Roman Empire, there is the *Historical Atlas of Central Europe* by Paul R. Magocsi (rev. and exp. ed., Seattle: Univ. of Washington Press, 2002).

Aside from names of cities and territories, Zeeden also uses vague geographical designations and names of regions not on the map. For example, Upper and Middle Baden are not well-defined terms and are not labeled, whereas the map shows specific boundaries for the Upper Palatinate and Lower and Upper Lusatia. In general, upper, middle, and lower refer to elevation, such as the plains of Lower Germany, the hills of Middle Germany, and the mountains of Upper Germany. *Mitteldeutschland* is always translated here as "central Germany" to avoid confusion with modern usage of the term "Middle Germany" as a region consisting of the modern states of Saxony, Thuringia, and Saxony-Anhalt. The map does not show borders for Thuringia, which was a region consisting of multiple territories in Saxony, bounded by Hesse (west), the Harz Mountains (north), the Saale River (east), and the Thuringian Forest (south). Likewise, the map does not show borders for Franconia, a region that consisted of various territories extending from the Thuringian Forest down to the Danube River and from Bohemia over to Frankfurt am Main. Lower Saxony does not appear on the map since it denotes a modern state in northwestern Germany.

One example of shifting boundaries is found in Ducal and Electoral Saxony. With the emperor's defeat of the Lutherans in the Smalcald War (1547), electorship was stripped from the Ernestine line and given to the Albertine line.[24] Thus prior to 1547, Electoral Saxony refers to the territory governed by Ernestine rulers and Ducal Saxony to that by Albertine. After the war, part of Electoral Saxony stayed in the electorate, passing from Ernestine to Albertine hands

---

[24] When Frederick II, Elector of Saxony, died in 1464, his two sons Ernest and Albert inherited his territories and ruled jointly. In 1485 they made a treaty and divided the territories, thereby separating the Wettin line into the Ernestine and Albertine lines. As the elder, Ernest retained the electorship, while Albert became a duke. In 1546 Duke Moritz (Albertine) invaded the lands of his cousin, Elector Johann Friedrich I, thereby betraying the Smalcald League and supporting Emperor Charles V. After defeating the Smalcald League in 1547, the emperor thanked Moritz by making him the Elector of Saxony and Johann Friedrich I the Duke of Saxony.

(KS and AS* on the map),[25] while the remainder became the Duchy of Saxony (Ernestine, ES on the map) or became part of Bohemia[26]; what had been the Duchy of Saxony now became part of the Electorate of Saxony (Albertine, AS on the map). More shifts occurred in 1554 with the death of Johann Friedrich I.

Here I would also like to express my thanks to Rev. Dr. Benjamin Mayes and Rev. Michael Frese, who provided the impetus for undertaking this translation years ago and rendered assistance, along with Pfarrer André Schneider. In revising this work for publication, I owe special thanks to Dr. Joseph Herl for his many comments suggesting improvements to the translation, preface, and notes. My notes are followed by my initials to distinguish them from the author's. I have also made additions in square brackets. Unless otherwise noted, translations of texts other than Zeeden's are my own.

The Fourth Week in Advent, 2011
Kevin G. Walker

---

[25] Much of this was the electoral district (*Kurkreis*) of Saxony (KS on the map), which included Wittenberg. Having lost this chief city and its university, Johann Friedrich I later planned the University of Jena and made Weimar his capital. For more information about the electoral district of Saxony, see the source by Schmidt below in note 407 and the dissertation of one of Zeeden's doctoral students, Gunter Tietz, *Das Erscheinungsbild von Pfarrstand und Pfarrgemeinde des sächsischen Kurkreises im Spiegel der Visitationsberichte des 16. Jahrhunderts* (Tübingen, 1971).

[26] Vogtland (marked on the map by the city Plauen) had been part of Electoral Saxony, but the emperor gave it to his chancellor. Twelve years later (1559) it effectively became part of Electoral Saxony again due to unpaid debts.

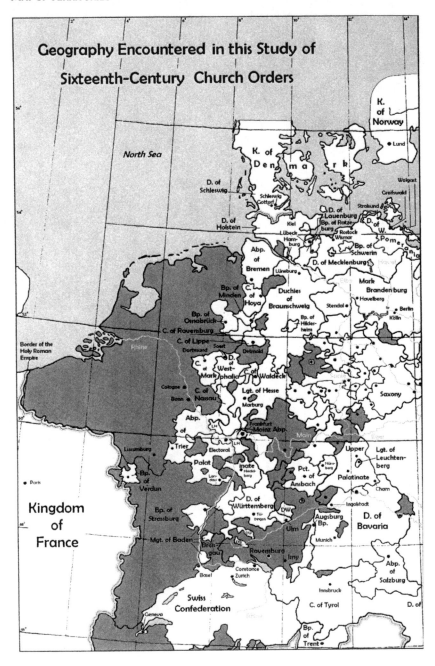

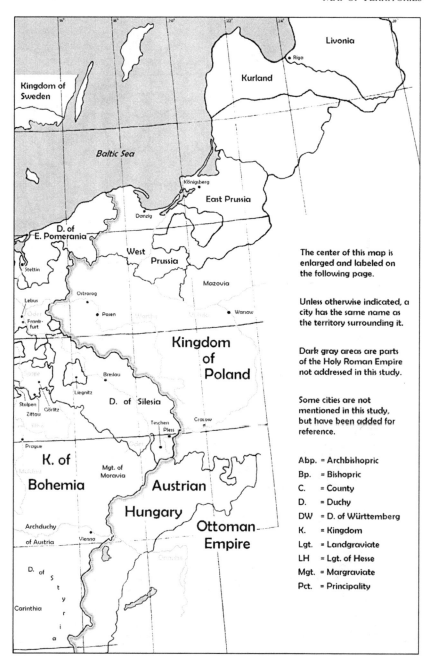

Livonia

Riga

Kurland

Kingdom of
Sweden

Baltic Sea

Königsberg

East Prussia

Danzig

D. of
E. Pomerania

Stettin

West
Prussia

Mazovia

Lebus

Ostrorog

Posen

Warsaw

Frank-
furt

Kingdom
of
Poland

Breslau

Liegnitz

Stolpen
Zittau   Görlitz

D. of Silesia

Teschen
Pless

Cracow

Prague

K. of

Mgt. of
Moravia

Bohemia

Austrian

Hungary

Archduchy

of Austria

Vienna

Ottoman
Empire

D.   of
S
t
y
r
i
a

Carinthia

The center of this map is
enlarged and labeled on
the following page.

Unless otherwise indicated, a
city has the same name as
the territory surrounding it.

Dark gray areas are parts
of the Holy Roman Empire
not addressed in this study.

Some cities are not
mentioned in this study,
but have been added for
reference.

Abp. = Archbishopric

Bp. = Bishopric

C.   = County

D.   = Duchy

DW = D. of Württemberg

K.   = Kingdom

Lgt. = Landgraviate

LH = Lgt. of Hesse

Mgt. = Margraviate

Pct. = Principality

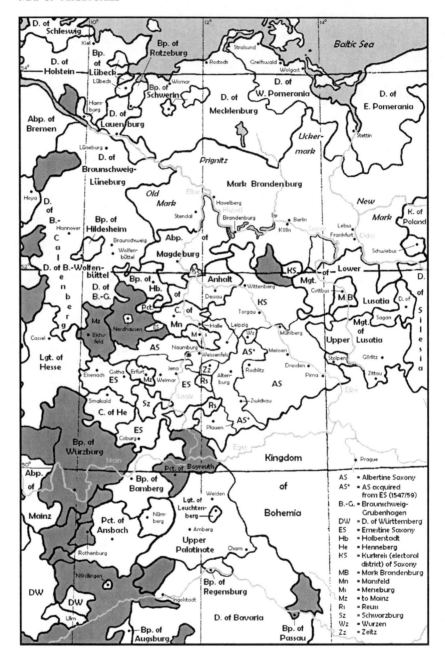

PREFACE

Since *Catholic* traditions in Lutheran church orders shall be spoken of in the investigation submitted here, it will be expedient to indicate in a few words what is meant by Catholic, so as not to evoke any misunderstandings. Here, Catholic means and can mean nothing other than ecclesiastical tradition from the period prior to the Reformation. In this regard, "ecclesiastical" should be understood quite broadly, and it should not be forgotten that many things in the late medieval church, which was notoriously quite liberal with regard to religious views and their discussion, looked different from post-Tridentine Catholicism.[27] Moreover, the "Catholic" that shall be spoken of here does not refer much at all to the doctrine, but rather to the outer garment of the church. We wish to observe what of this remained beyond the Reformation[28] in the cities and territories that had become evangelical[29]: in the divine service, in devotional and religious customs, in law, and in the realm of church polity.

Even longer and more intensive research is required before any clear and unquestionable results concerning the material treated here can be submitted. What *this* investigation offers is a preliminary survey at best; it cannot yet provide a sufficient picture, but must be content with intimations and references. This study, which arose from long occupation with the Lutheran church orders, makes no claim to completeness or general validity of the statements submitted and also refrains from drawing far-reaching conclusions based on the facts ascertained. Its sole purpose is to make known that certain Catholic

---

[27] That is, Roman Catholicism after the Council of Trent, which took place from 1545–1563. – KGW

[28] When Zeeden refers to the Reformation as a point in time, he appears to mean the presentation of the Augsburg Confession in 1530 (see Chapter 3, II. c). – KGW

[29] As a rule, the word "evangelical" in this book can be equated with "Lutheran" rather than Protestant in general, those in the Reformed Church, or the sense of any later "evangelical" movements. Zeeden begins his introduction speaking generally, but then limits the study to the Lutheran Church, with only occasional references to the Reformed. – KGW

traditions *did* remain, what they looked like, and where they were encountered.

This little work goes back to a presentation made before members of the Society for Publishing the Corpus Catholicorum and the historical division of the Görres Society on Sept. 30, 1958 in Salzburg. My special thanks go to Prof. Dr. Hubert Jedin for his ever stimulating consultation and for the favor of receiving this study in the series of publications of the Society for Publishing the Corpus Catholicorum. Thanks are due to cand. phil. Andrea Wiedeburg, Tübingen, and Dr. Horst Rabe, likewise in Tübingen, for help reading the drafts. But I owe especial thanks to Dr. Rabe for kindly taking pains to compile the indexes for people, places, and subjects.

Tübingen, July 8, 1959.

Ernst Walter Zeeden.

ABBREVIATIONS

BSLK   = *Die Bekenntnisschriften der evangelisch-lutherischen Kirche.* (2nd ed.) Göttingen: Vandenhoeck & Ruprecht, 1952.

CR   = *Corpus Reformatorum: Philippi Melanthonis Opera quae supersunt omnia.* (ed. by Karl Gottlieb Bretschneider; Heinrich Ernst Bindseil) Halis Saxonum: C. A. Schwetschke et filium, 1834–60.

Delius = Delius, Walter. "Die kirchlichen Zustände der Reformationszeit im Amt Querfurt nach den Kirchenvisitationsakten von 1555, 1563 und 1583." *Zeitschrift des Vereins für Kirchengeschichte der Provinz Sachsen und des Freistaates Anhalt* 30 (1934): 79–90.

Drews   = Drews, Paul. *Beiträge zu Luthers liturgischen Reformen.* (*Studien zur Geschichte des Gottesdienstes und des gottesdienstlichen Lebens IV/V*) Tübingen: J. C. B. Mohr (Paul Siebeck), 1910.

DWB   = *Deutsches Worterbuch.* ed. by Jacob and Wilhelm Grimm. 32 vols. Leipzig: S. Hirzel, 1854–1961.

Feddersen = Feddersen, Ernst. *Kirchengeschichte Schleswig-Holsteins II: 1517–1721.* (*Schriften des Vereins für Schleswig-Holsteinische Kirchengeschichte* 19) Kiel: Mühlau, 1938.

Fendt   = Fendt, Leonhard. *Der lutherische Gottesdienst des 16. Jahrhunderts: sein Werden und sein Wachsen.* München: Ernst Reinhardt, 1923.

Götz, *Bewegung* = Götz, Johann Baptist. *Die religiöse Bewegung in der Oberpfalz von 1520 bis 1560.* (*Erläuterungen und Ergänzungen zu Janssens Geschichte des deutschen Volkes* 10, 1–2) Freiburg im Breisgau: Herder, 1914.

Götz, *Einf.* = Götz, Johann Baptist. *Die erste Einführung des Kalvinismus in der Oberpfalz, 1559–1576.* (*Reformationsgeschichtliche Studien und Texte* 60) Münster i. W.: Aschendorff, 1933.

Götz, *Wirren* = Götz, Johann Baptist. *Die religiösen Wirren in der Oberpfalz von 1576 bis 1620.* (*Reformationsgeschichtliche Studien und Texte* 66) Münster i. W.: Aschendorff, 1937.

Graff = Graff, Paul. *Geschichte der Auflösung der alten gottesdienstlichen Formen in der evangelischen Kirche Deutschlands.* (2nd ed.) Göttingen: Vandenhoeck & Ruprecht, 1937.

Heckel = Heckel, Johannes. *Die evangelischen Dom- und Kollegiatstifter Preussens.* Kirchenrechtliche Abhandlungen 100/101) Stuttgart: F. Enke, 1924.

Liber Usualis = *The Liber Usualis: With Introduction and Rubrics in English,* ed. by the Benedictines of Solesmes, Tournai; New York: Desclee Company, 1961.

LSB = *Lutheran Service Book.* The Commission on Worship of The Lutheran Church—Missouri Synod. Saint Louis: Concordia Publishing House, 2006.

Lund = Lund, Eric, ed. *Documents from the History of Lutheranism, 1517–1750.* Minneapolis: Fortress Press, 2002.

LW = *Luther's Works.* ed. by Jaroslav Pelikan et al. Philadephia: Fortress Press; Saint Louis: Concordia Publishing House, 1955–.

Müller = Müller, Nikolaus "Zur Geschichte des Gottesdienstes der Domkirche zu Berlin in den Jahren 1540–1598." *Jahrbuch für branden-burgische Kirchengeschichte* 2/3 (1906): 337–551.

Nottarp = Nottarp, Hermann. *Zur Communicatio in sacris cum haereticis.* (*Schriften der Königsberger Gelehrten Gesellschaft. Geisteswissenschaftliche Klasse.* 9, 4) Halle: Niemeyer, 1933.

Plantiko	= Plantiko, Otto. *Pommersche Reformationsgeschichte.* Greifswald: L. Bamberg, 1922.
Ramge	= Ramge, Karl. *Das gottesdienstliche und kulturell-sittliche Leben des alten lutherischen Amberg 1538–1626/28.* Neuendettelsau: Freimund-Verlag, 1938.
RGG	= *Religion in Geschichte und Gegenwart: Handwörterbuch für Theologie und Religionswissenschaft.* (2nd ed.) Tübingen: J. C. B. Mohr, 1927–1932.
Richter	= Richter, Aemilius Ludwig, ed. *Die evangelischen Kirchenordnungen des 16. Jahrhunderts.* 2 vols. Weimar: Landes-Industriecomptoir, 1846.
Schmidt	= Schmidt, Wilhelm. "Die Bremer evangelische Messe 1525," in *Hospitium Ecclesiae, Forschungen zur Bremischen Kirchengeschichte,* ed. by Bodo Heyne and Kurd Schulz (Bremen: Boettcher, 1954): 52–85.
Sehling	= Sehling, Emil, ed. *Die evangelischen Kirchenordnungen des XVI. Jahrhunderts,* vols. 1–5, Aalen: Scientia Verlag, 1970–79, vols. 6ff. Tübingen: J. C. B. Mohr (Paul Siebeck), 1957–.
WA	= *D. Martin Luthers Werke: kritische Gesamtausgabe.* Weimar: H. Böhlau, 1883–.
Wilken	= Wilken, Johannes. *Die niederdeutschen evangelischen Kirchenordnungen des 16. Jahrhunderts als Quelle zur deutschen Kulturgeschichte.* Diss. phil. Hamburg, 1927.

INTRODUCTION

THE EVANGELICAL CHURCH ORDERS

The church orders are tied most intimately to the organization of the evangelical church, which proved to be necessary shortly after the Reformation; taken as a whole, they document the beginnings and later phases of evangelical church formation. Everywhere the Reformation found entrance, internal considerations necessitated reorganization of the church polity, and not this alone, but along with it also the church law and worship. Everything—polity, worship, and law—had to be transformed or reshaped in such a way that it was consonant with the new doctrine or at least did not contradict it. The way for doing so was led by those lands within Germany that were first in turning to the Reformation, such as the Ernestine Electorate of Saxony, Hesse, and the Franconian margraviates or the city of Hamburg.

The evangelical church polity grew as a rule upon the foundation of the state, territory, or even city in some cases. The preconditions for this are to be sought in the established church of the late Middle Ages. On account of being bound to territories and the great number of these territories, evangelical churches attained all sorts of different forms of polity. Despite the particularities that come to light, there are unmistakable common traits, especially within churches of the same confessional basis. For instance, the most general principal traits of all Protestant churches include the concept of leading the church in need of reform back to Holy Scripture, separation from the papacy, abolition of hierarchy, and reduction of the number of sacraments. Much still remained, at least at first, from the medieval past, such as the concept of ecclesial unity, the intimate connection between church and state which evolved over time, the mutual permeation of church and world, and the fundamental intolerance, which, however, was implemented more strictly now in the course of the religious battles.

Luther's writings after 1517 and especially since 1520 treated from various, mostly practical angles, the question of how and according to which points of view the church ought to be reformed. The primary thought was that it should be purified so that the Gospel could be preached within it freely. In this regard, "freely" meant according to Luther's doctrine. Among the guidelines that he issued, his preface to Melanchthon's "Instruction for the Visitors in the Electorate of Saxony" (1528)[30] stands at the threshold of the evangelical state or territorial church. Luther acknowledged in this that his electoral prince has authority to carry out organizational reform of [the church in] his electorate, though with weighty reservations and under certain conditions tied to current events.[31] One condition indicated by Luther was that the rightful ecclesial authority of the bishops had failed and was unfit for carrying out reform. His reservations referred to this condition: Only as a substitute for the rightful, but unfit bearer of spiritual authority is he [the elector/prince] to assume leadership of the church, as an emergency bishop or, in a sense, as a delegated representative. Within the Christian community he is the foremost member, therefore this office falls to him in his capacity as a member of the community. However, the prince should have no power *over the office of preaching the Word*; this should be independent from his office.

The prince thought somewhat differently than Luther on this point. Elector Johann the Steadfast undertook the organizational reform of the church by virtue of his own title, exercising the sovereignty over the church[32] in his realm due him as prince. And so with the electoral visitation instruction of 1527[33] began de facto the sovereign church government, i.e. the era "in which the prince also issued worship and doctrinal ordinances in exercise of his hitherto existing sovereignty over the church, in which he also assumed the

---

[30] Luther's preface and the "Instruction" are in *LW* 40:263–320. – KGW

[31] See *LW* 40:271–3, where Luther describes the appeal to and obligation of the elector. Sehling (1:33) notes that it was neither Luther's idea to have visitations nor his desire to have the secular authorities interfere with "the purely religious movement." Only after seeing the great need did he begin to break with his ideal of leaving the church free to develop, unbound by laws, and desire aid from the secular realm in the form of visitations. – KGW

[32] Sovereignty over the church = *Kirchenhoheit*, the equivalent of the Latin term *ius circa sacra* (also *jus, iura,* or *jura*). This is the sovereign right of the ruler/state in matters of the church, which generally includes the right to protect or act as patron (*jus advocatiae, jus protectionis*), the right to reform or allow the presence of a church (*jus reformandi, jus receptionis*), and the right of superintendence (*jus supremae inspectionis*). – KGW

[33] This document is in Sehling 1:142–8. – KGW

now headless episcopal jurisdiction together with doctrinal authority, in which he installed church officials in his own name" (Leopold Zscharnack in *RGG* vol. 3, p. 1010).

The organization of the evangelical church, at least insofar as it has to do with Lutheranism, is therefore intimately connected with the rise of a stricter governance. But this is much different from the ordinances of the Calvinist church. The difference concerns the structure as well as the relation to the state. This becomes quite clear in the following three points: 1. the Calvinistic church builds itself from the congregation up; 2. it regards itself as principally independent in relation to the state; 3. next to doctrine and worship, it puts the greatest emphasis on strict church discipline and moral discipline and develops its own organs to enforce this.

In western Europe—not including England—Calvinism became the dominant form of Protestantism, likewise in Switzerland and parts of western Germany. Otherwise Lutheranism prevailed in Germany and in its eastern and southeastern neighbors; in Scandinavia it dominated without competition. When viewed more closely, deeply rooted differences between the Reformed (Calvinistic) and the Lutheran church orders can be observed. In our presentation, which deals particularly with German conditions, we refrain from looking at the Reformed Church and restrict ourselves to the organization of the church in sixteenth-century Lutheranism, namely in its manifestation where Lutheranism had spread most vigorously in northern, eastern, and central Germany.

This organization was reflected in the church orders. They were the foundational church laws. They were, at least generally, issued by the political authorities, the princes, cities, and baronies. The authorities usually allowed themselves to be advised for this purpose, sometimes by Luther himself, often by leading men of the Reformation. In many cases, the orders were drafted by Lutheran theologians; in effect, they shaped the Lutheran church wherever the orders were adopted. But these orders did not become legally binding until the political authorities concerned issued them in their names. Details pertaining to the legal force and duration of church orders differed—but we will not dwell on that here (cf. Erich Foerster's "Kirchenordnung" article in *RGG* vol. 3). There are church orders from the sixteenth century, for example, that remain valid in individual parts up to the present within some German territorial

3

churches (for example the 1536 church order for the city of Hannover; Sehling 6/2:941). They were issued under various names in those days, such as church orders, religion mandates, instructions, etc. Often they also contained a school order. Sometimes they even appeared as a portion of a more comprehensive territorial order or policy order.[34] In the great majority of cases they specifically pertained to the *credenda* and *agenda*: doctrine (in summary form, and usually bound with a catechism) and the liturgy. In addition, often there were also provisions for church finances, spiritual jurisdiction, establishing additional ecclesiastical offices, and visitation procedures; further, there were admonitions to parsons and congregations concerning moral lifestyle as well as pertinent provisions for punishment.[35] Here the church order already borders on the type of moral mandate associated with the ordinances of city and state authorities most used in the sixteenth and seventeenth centuries. In these, those who bore authority made punishable offenses of drunkenness and gluttony by clergy and laity, desecration of Sunday by working, visiting a tavern or brandy shop during the chief service, and the like with patient regularity. At the same time, the persistent repetition of these things gives a sense of how powerless people were in opposition to these occurrences. On various occasions separate

---

[34] A policy order (*Polizeiordnung*) is a book containing public policies and ordinances. For more information and resources concerning policy orders and ordinances, cf. John Witte, Jr. *Law and Protestantism: The Legal Teachings of the Lutheran Reformation* (Cambridge University Press, 2002), p. 183f. note 16. – KGW

[35] Lund (p. 124f.) describes these two parts of church orders a little more fully and names the third: "The first section usually concerned *Credenda*, or what ought to be believed. It described the doctrines that were considered normative for the churches and often specified what local church workers ought to do to ensure that the people understood and accepted these teachings. The second section, concerning *Agenda*, or what ought to be done, described the liturgy the churches would follow and set forth other regulations for the celebration of church rites. The third section, *Administranda*, focused on how the churches ought to be organized. It outlined the duties and qualifications of church workers, clarified how the church should relate to civil government, and related the ministry of the churches to other work such as the educating of the young and care for the poor." – KGW

orders for monasteries and cathedrals were also issued for the purpose of introducing evangelical services there.

Well over a thousand such orders were published between the beginning of the Reformation and the end of the Thirty Years' War (about 1522–1648). But even after the Peace of Westphalia, this form of church legislation did not stop any time soon. The tide first began to fall slowly in the eighteenth century. The physical extent of the church orders varied; some contained only a few pages, others several hundred. The main works were made accessible for central and eastern Germany by the five-volume publication of Emil Sehling, 1902–1913; the orders for the western part of northern and central Germany are being published successively since 1955. It is on this material that the following accounts are based. Of the extant sixteenth-century church orders, an overwhelming number, about two-thirds to three-quarters, stem from the second half of the century. This serves to document a fact that can also be known by other means—a fact that apparently has not yet fully penetrated our historical consciousness—, that the institutional consolidation or church formation of Protestantism, to a certain extent the second, conservative phase of the Reformation in Germany, actually occurs after the Religious Peace of Augsburg (1555) and accordingly belongs in the time period that we conventionally designate as the age of the Counter-Reformation, even if this is not entirely accurate with regard to time and relevant issues.

CHAPTER 1

THE SERVICES
AND OTHER ACTS OF WORSHIP

The church orders often emphasize how they differ from the papacy. Occasionally they also comment on a usage or rite to the effect that they want it understood evangelically rather than "papistically"; for example, the tolling of the *Ave* bell, the solemn introduction of a woman into the church six weeks after having given birth (churching), or the celebration of a festival for a city's patron saint. However, a great deal of what appears to us moderns from the distance of 400 years as truly Catholic was not commented on at all, but regarded as matter of course, or sometimes the remark was added that it pertained to a good Christian custom that had been in effect for ages in the land or city concerned; for example, tax exemption and the *privilegium fori*[36] for clergy, for whom, moreover, the word "priest" was still in vogue. Such "matters of course" shall be dealt with in what follows. Forms and examples of isolated or unusual faithfulness to tradition, which are not to be regarded as typical but occurred nevertheless, shall not be omitted. They will also be dealt with, yet the radius of their validity will be noted as accurately as possible and they will be identified as having existed in particular churches, places, or territories.

Among other service forms preserved from the Catholic period and living on in Lutheranism today are the Mass, Matins, and Vespers; various meditations and prayers, among which is the Litany

---

[36] The privilege of the forum: Clergy were exempt from the jurisdiction of civil courts and were instead tried by ecclesiastical courts. – KGW

for All Saints; the rites for administering the sacraments, and a number of half-liturgical, half-popular expressions of piety, such as processions. Moreover, the service was carried out in hitherto Catholic churches with little or no change to its furnishings and appearance at first. The services fell in line with the rhythm of the ancient Catholic church year with its seasons, like Advent, Lent, and Passiontide, with its high feasts and saints' days, its patron saint festivals, and church dedications. Of course that did not all cross over into the new confession without changes. The usury of the late Middle Ages in worship and veneration of saints was cut and liturgical expressions of piety were reduced to a level with biblical support. The administration of the sacraments and the ceremonies associated with them experienced this or that alteration according to the theology of the Reformation. Nevertheless, an amazing amount remained from the outward form and flow of the Catholic service, and that not only from the outward sides of medieval worship, but also from the substance of traditional piety, for example from elements of the *Ordo Missae* (the Order of the Mass or ordinaries) and from the prayers of the church.

In the following we will first consider tradition to the extent that it was received into evangelical services, then that which remained from it in sacramental practice and in other religious customs. An overview of days, times, and types of services is placed at the beginning.

I. THE SERVICE AND ITS CHIEF FORMS

A. DAILY SERVICES

First of all, it should be noted here that early Lutheranism was acquainted with daily services as a matter of principle. Sundays were observed, as far as possible, with Matins and the chief service (the service with the Lord's Supper) in the morning, and with a catechism sermon or catechism instruction and Vespers in the afternoon. Insofar as they were sung, the weekday[37] services, whose roots can be seen in the Catholic daily service,[38] were generally carried by Latin school students in cities having these; the services consisted of Matins and

[37] Weekdays (*Wochentage*) and workdays (*Werktage*) meant Monday through Saturday in the sixteenth century. – KGW
[38] Graff 1:215.

Vespers, and therefore were essentially liturgical. In larger cities a daily sermon[39] or summaries[40] and the Litany might also have been included. In the country, where there were no advanced school students, if a preaching service could not take place on Wednesday and Friday, prayer hours were to be held at the minimum. Saturday was designated as a day for confession.[41] The week was to be a miniature mirror of the church year, with Sunday recalling the Resurrection, Wednesday and Friday the Passion Week.[42] In many places, such as Amberg, Regensburg, Nürnberg, and Magdeburg, the so-called Tenebrae was sung during Matins on Fridays with solemn bell tolls in remembrance of Christ's death as in the Catholic period.[43] On Thursdays in Nürnberg and Amberg, a Mount of Olives devotion that had grown from the Maundy Thursday Matins was observed; responsories and bell tolling in this devotion fostered thoughts of

---

[39] Or, as far as possible, on *a few* days during the week.

[40] These summaries or glosses took on various forms, the most popular being those of Veit Dietrich, which covered the Old and New Testaments (*Summaria vber die gantze Bibel, das alte vnd newe Testament*, Nürnberg, 1545). See Robert Kolb's article, "The *Summaria* of Veit Dietrich as an Aid for Teaching the Faith" in *Archiv für Reformationsgeschichte / Archive for Reformation History* 99 (2008): 97–119. In addition to summarizing nearly every chapter of the Bible, Dietrich briefly described the main points to be learned from them. Rather than write his own summaries for the psalms, in his first edition for the Old Testament (*Summaria über das alte Testament*, Wittenberg, 1541) he simply referred to the "Summaries of the Psalms" written by Luther (*Summarien über die Psalmen*, Wittenberg, 1531, *WA* 38:17–69), a translation of which is to appear in the American Edition of Luther's Works by Concordia Publishing House. Another form of summaries appeared anonymously the year before Dietrich's Old Testament summary and similarly went through numerous editions and republications (*Evangelia mit den Summarien, vnd Epistel, Auff alle Sontage vnd fürnemesten Feste, durch das gantze jar*, Leipzig, 1540). It included the Epistle and Gospel readings (sometimes an Old Testament reading) for all the Sundays and primary festivals in the church year, each Gospel reading being followed by a brief summary and commentary with related Bible passages. – KGW

[41] Graff 1:111f.

[42] Graff 1:111f.

[43] Ramge, 97; Graff 1:111f. with sources and references; likewise the 1534 Harzgerode church order, Sehling 2:586f.; the Tenebrae remain in the Upper Palatinate despite severe Calvinistic countermeasures; Götz, *Wirren*, 237, 343.

Christ sweating blood.[44] The tradition of Catholic votive masses lived on in the numerous evangelical penitential services; thus the corresponding evangelical service orders[45] knew masses for peace, for rain and good weather, and for remission of sins (*pro pace, pro pluvia et serenitate, pro remissione peccatorum*).[46] Aside from this, the evangelical weekday services were particularly structured in accordance with an occasion or time of the church year; the Ember Days and Lent, for example, profoundly bolstered doctrine by means of catechism sermons.[47]

B. THE EVANGELICAL MASS, MATINS, AND VESPERS

Concerning the chief service on Sundays, this retained the name Office or Mass. This remained its designation in northern Germany into the eighteenth century. The most important impetus for evangelically recasting the Mass came from Luther, but various efforts in the same direction can also be observed before and alongside him.[48] Luther expressed himself concerning this in three particular works: *On the Order of the Service in the Congregation*, 1523; *An Order of Mass* (*Formula Missae*) etc., 1523; *The German Mass* (*Deutsche Messe*), 1526.[49] The theological thought of purifying the Mass of components contrary to the evangelical understanding of salvation and the pastoral thought of making it simpler and understandable for the people by using the German language acted as touchstones for these changes. With the German form, however, the Latin form was by no means to disappear categorically. On the contrary, it was expressly provided for in especially solemn services and for cities. Alongside traditional considerations, of course, pedagogical considerations also carried decisive weight: Schoolboys were to practice Latin while singing psalms, hymns, and the like with the choir.

---

[44] Ramge, 95.

[45] For example, the *Cantica sacra, quo ordine et melodiis, per totius anni curriculum, in matutinis & vespertinis, itemq[ue] intermedijs precibus cantari solent* (Magdeburg 1613).

[46] Graff 1:236.

[47] The 1569 Wolfenbüttel church order, Sehling 6/1:153f. [For more on the Ember Days and Lent, see part IV below.]

[48] Julius Smend, *Die evangelischen deutschen Messen bis zu Luthers deutscher Messe* (Göttingen: Vandenhoeck, 1896).

[49] *WA* 12:31, 205ff., and 19:44ff. [*LW* 53:7–14, 15–40, 51–90.]

According to many reports, both the German language and the changing of the service in connection with the evangelical sermon signified a tangible innovation for the 1520's. As one voice among many we refer here to the report of the Bremen Chronicle concerning the beginning of the Reformation in the city Bremen: "1525. In this year, a great change in ceremonies has occurred in Bremen's churches, for the Latin hymns have been changed into German psalms, the four parish churches assimilated virtually one after the other, the holy Gospel is taught purely in them, the ungodly, papistical ceremonies and hymns have been totally removed and Christian hymns have been prescribed and adopted in their place, Holy Baptism in the German language has been sanctioned, also the venerable holy Sacrament of Jesus Christ's body and blood is administered in both kinds to every single Christian, according to the Lord Christ's institution and His holy last will."[50]

From the view of the Bremen chronicler, the evangelical celebration of the Mass certainly presents a striking innovation, compared with the liturgy of the ancient church.[51] On the other hand, seen through the eyes of a Reformed Upper German preacher, it signified a strong bit of papacy nonetheless. In May of 1536, the Reformed clergyman Wolfgang Musculus, who hailed from the Strasbourg Reformation and now worked in Augsburg, stayed in Eisenach for a couple of days on account of his trip to the Wittenberg Concord meetings[52] and there attended a Lutheran Sunday service. He described how it went. His report is one of the few contemporary

---

[50] "Auszüge aus Chroniken" in *Bremisches Jahrbuch*, Second series, vol. 1, p. 228: *Quellen zur Bremischen Reformationsgeschichte* (1885). [This is also quoted in Schmidt, 54–55, who notes that at that time, and for a long time after, "psalms" generally referred to spiritual songs, even if they were not metrical psalms. Schmidt also names the four parish churches: Our Dear Lady, St. Ansgar, St. Martin, St. Stephan.]

[51] Likewise from the view of a Roman Catholic; cf. for example the remarks of a Westphalian oblate [i.e. lay brother, Göbel von Köln] concerning the evangelical service in the city of Braunschweig, 1527, 1528, and 1529: Klemens Löffler, "Aus den Aufzeichnungen eines westfälischen Klosterbruders der Reformationszeit," *Zeitschrift der Gesellschaft für niedersächsische Kirchengeschichte* 18 (1913), 140ff.

[52] Walther Köhler, *Zwingli und Luther: Ihr Streit über das Abendmahl nach seinen politischen und religiösen Beziehungen*, vol. 2, p. 443 (Gütersloh: Bertelsmann, 1953).

depictions dealing with the practical implementation of the Lutheran Mass. But it is also especially valuable and interesting because the one rendering the report possessed a keener eye, from the distance of the Reformed, for the elements in the Lutheran liturgy that were specifically Catholic. Musculus' description reads:

"At 7:00 we entered the church[53] where the Office of the Mass, as they call it, was held in the following manner:

"First the boys and the headmaster sang the Introit for Cantate Sunday in Latin, set apart in the chancel in an entirely papistical fashion. Then came the Kyrie eleison with the organ being played in alternation. Thirdly a deacon, dressed entirely according to the papistical fashion and standing by the altar, which was likewise adorned with candles and other things, sang in Latin 'Gloria in excelsis Deo' (Glory to God in the highest); this canticle the choir and organist again completed. When this was finished the deacon sang a collect, as they call it, in German, facing the altar with his back turned toward the congregation, and appended a reading from the Epistle of James, facing the congregation, also in German.

"Again the organ was played while the choir sang, 'Victimae paschali' and the congregation sang responsively, 'Christ ist erstanden!'[54]

"Upon this the deacon sang a portion of the Gospel in German, 'But now I am going to Him who sent Me,' etc. (John 16:5), while facing the congregation. After this reading the organ was played as the congregation sang, 'We All Believe in One True God.'[55]

---

[53] Zeeden has the following remark in brackets: of the Franciscans in Eisenach. – KGW

[54] For "Victimae paschali," see "Christians, to the Paschal Victim," LSB 460 (the music is in the LSB Hymn Accompaniment Edition, but not the Pew Edition) or canticle 10 in Lutheran Worship (St. Louis: Concordia Publishing House, 1982); for "Christ ist erstanden," see "Christ Is Arisen," LSB 459 or Lutheran Worship 10. For the Latin text, see Liber Usualis, p. 780. – KGW

[55] LSB 954. The German title is "Wir glauben all' an einen Gott." – KGW

"When this was finished Justus Menius preached, dressed in the usual manner, not in any special robe.[56]

"After the sermon the deacon, standing at the altar in priestly garb, exhorted the people to prayer for some particularly enumerated concerns and closed with Christ's promise: 'Whatever you ask the Father,' etc. (John 15:16, 16:23). Next he briefly recalled the institution of the Lord's Supper, then he sang the Words of Institution first over the bread, whereby he elevated it entirely according to the papistical fashion while genuflecting away from the people; then over the chalice, which he likewise elevated after finishing the Words of Institution. When this was over the organ played and the choir sang the Agnus Dei (Lamb of God). Meanwhile Communion began. A deacon dressed in the usual manner administered the chalice. Not a single man was seen going to Communion, but a few little women were communed. Following this, the deacon communed himself at the altar, after having first adored the bread,[57] although he did not do so with the chalice. This he carefully emptied and then washed with newly poured wine, so that nothing of the blood remained.

"After Communion he sang a prayer while facing the altar. When this was finished he dismissed the people with a benediction that he sang while facing them.

"Finally, as the congregation left the church the choir sang *Da pacem, Domine*[58] in German. And with that this celebration was ended.

"Vespers was held at 1:00 in the afternoon, entirely after the papistical fashion, in the chancel, except that a boy sang the Sunday Gospel down to the congregation from the loft in the ordinary manner. After Vespers there was a sermon on the

---

[56] Instead of "dressed" to the period, Zeeden has ellipses and the following remark in brackets: in a black academic's robe. – KGW

[57] Zeeden has the following remark in brackets: by genuflecting. – KGW

[58] "Grant Peace, We Pray, in Mercy Lord," *LSB* 777–8. The German title is *"Verleih' uns Frieden gnädiglich,"* *WA* 35:232–5, 458. For the Latin text, see *Liber Usualis*, p. 1867f. – KGW

Second Commandment, 'You shall not take the name of the Lord your God in vain,' etc., after which 'Christ is arisen' was sung."[59]

The report, which essentially agrees with the majority of Lutheran church orders and agendas of the sixteenth century, lets us see roughly what fell away from the Roman Mass and what remained. The deletions concerned the sacrifice of the Mass, the offertory and the prayers that followed it, as well as the Canon of the Mass, except for the consecration. As can be ascertained from the pertinent works of Luther, however, the presentation of bread and wine was essentially retained.[60] Generally the preface with the Sanctus and

---

[59] *Analecta Lutherana: Briefe und Actenstücke zur Geschichte Luthers*, ed. by Theodor Kolde (Gotha: Perthes, 1883), 216ff.; I follow the German translation of Rudolf Herrmann, *Thüringische Kirchengeschichte* vol. 2, p. 112f. (Weimar: Hermann Böhlaus Nachfolger, 1947). [I have made many adjustments based on the original Latin in Kolde. Note that "deacon" appears here where "*Diakon*" is in the German and "*minister*" is in the Latin.] Cf. also Wolfgang Musculus' description of a service in Wittenberg in Kolde, 226ff.

[60] Cf. *Formula Missae*; also Schmidt, 75. [Zeeden may be referring to the following passages in the *Formula Missae*: "Now the additions of the early fathers who, it is reported, softly prayed one or two Psalms before blessing the bread and wine are commendable." "After the Creed or after the sermon let bread and wine be made ready for blessing in the customary manner." *LW* 53:20 and 26, cf. *WA* 12:206 lines 23–25 and 211 lines 23–24. Note that the second passage immediately follows a repudiation of the sacrificial content and nature of the Roman Mass. Schmidt quotes (p. 74) a Eucharistic prayer from the Roman Missal (*Missale Romanum*) side-by-side with a similar prayer from the 1525 Evangelical Mass in Bremen and then writes (p. 75) that the main idea from the prayer has been taken over: "Calling upon God to have the bread and wine become the body and blood of Christ for us. . . . The significant theological weight of the epiclesis—which expresses that God alone is the doer in this—may have motivated Kantz and his Bremen successor to adopt precisely this prayer and only this prayer from the abundance of prayers in the Canon of the Mass. . . . For a Mass of the Reformation it is just as characteristic as it is natural that the word 'oblation' and all the adjectives associated with it are eliminated. Kantz and the Bremen Mass replace oblation with the words 'bread and wine,' which of course mean nothing other than that to which oblation refers. Thus merely the matter is introduced without using the name that has been customary since the time of the apostles." In the last two sentences here, Schmidt clearly disregards the connection between the word oblation and the Roman

Benedictus, as well as the Lord's Prayer, were also retained[61] in a more or less solemn form. Things were arranged differently with the preparatory prayers[62] prior to the service of prayer and instruction, i.e. with the parts that precede the Introit: Many church orders had the Mass begin right away with the Introit.[63] The Brandenburg church order of 1540 and 1572 placed the *Confiteor* at the beginning,[64] the influential Mecklenburg church order of 1552 began with general confession and absolution;[65] the Schwarzburg church order of 1574 began with singing *"Veni Sancte Spiritus"* in Latin (or in German if that was not possible).[66] The Bremen evangelical Mass from 1525 provided for an exhortation, an absolution of the congregation, a confession of the priest, a common invocation of the Holy Spirit, and a collect to the Holy Spirit. For this preparation for the service, which took the place of the preparatory prayers, it made use of numerous elements from the Roman Mass, for example fragments from the

---

Catholic understanding of the sacrifice of the Mass, which is something that the Reformation decidedly repudiated. Cf. *LW* 36:53f., where Luther associates the oblation with the elevation of the elements, but discounts the view of this as an offering or sacrifice (*WA* 6:524 line 21ff.). See also the Apology of the Augsburg Confession, Article XXIV.]

[61] As evidenced by the majority of church orders.

[62] *Staffelgebet*, also called *Stufengebet*, because the prayers at the beginning of the Mass were spoken by the celebrant before the steps to the altar. – KGW

[63] For example, Hoya 1581, Sehling 6/2:925; Northeim 1539, Sehling 6/2:1148; Lüneburg 1564, Sehling 6/1:542.

[64] Sehling 3:68 and 96. [*"Confiteor"* means "I confess" and refers to the priest's confession of sins at the beginning of the Mass. Lutherans modified it and soon began using it for general confession. Cf. pp. 358–371 of *Lutheran Worship: History and Practice*, ed. by Fred L. Precht (St. Louis: Concordia Publishing House, 1993), and the notes referring to church orders including the *Confiteor* or a form of general confession.]

[65] Sehling 5:197f.

[66] Sehling 2:132. ["Come, Holy Ghost, God and Lord," *LSB* 497. For the Latin text, see *Liber Usualis*, p. 885f. The Schwarzburg dominions were protectorates of Albertine Saxony in Thuringia. This church order is for the Upper County of Schwarzburg, which included the city of Schwarzburg, and in this year was divided into the counties of Schwarzburg-Arnstadt and Schwarzburg-Rudolstadt.]

formula for absolution, from the hymn *"Veni Creator Spiritus,"*[67] and from the sacrifice of the Mass; its collects were taken from the formulas for the week of Pentecost.[68]

If we ask what remained of the body of the Roman Mass, we find in the Lutheran service basically entire components from the Introit to the Creed, namely: the Kyrie, Gloria, collect, reading or Epistle, gradual, tract, sequence, Gospel. Afterwards the more severe abridgments set in. The preface, consecration words, Our Father (without its continuation *Libera nos*[69]), and Agnus Dei were retained. Some conservative church orders preserved the prayers before and after Communion; thus the church orders of the Brandenburg Electorate from 1540 and 1572 contained the *Domine Jesu Christe, qui dixisti*[70]; the *Domine Jesu Christe, fili Dei vivi*[71]; and the *Sacramentum* (instead of *Perceptio*) *corporis tui, domine Jesu Christe* (with minor linguistic modifications)[72]; also the *Corpus tuum*

---

[67] For the Latin text of this sequence, see *Liber Usualis*, p. 880f. A partial English translation is "Come, Holy Ghost, in Love," no. 11 in *Evangelical Lutheran Hymnary* (St. Louis: MorningStar Music Publishers, 1996). Other versions include Edward Caswall's "Holy Spirit, Lord of Light" and John Mason Neale's "Come, Thou Holy Paraclete," both of which appear in numerous hymnals. – KGW

[68] Schmidt, 65–71.

[69] These are the first two words of the prayer in the Canon of the Mass that directly follows the petition, "but deliver us from evil. Amen." Luther made this omission in his 1523 *Formula Missae*, explaining what he wanted in its place; cf. Sehling 1:6, *WA* 12:213 line 4ff., and *LW* 53:28 (paragraph V), which has an English translation of the prayer. Although Luther does not say so here, clearly the prayer's reference to the intercession of Mary and other saints was unacceptable. Latin and English in parallel for this and the following prayers can be found, for example, in the *Saint Andrew Daily Missal* ed. by Gaspar Lefebvre (Bruges: Biblica, 1962). – KGW

[70] This is the first prayer after the Agnus Dei, followed immediately by the next two. The two after that are post-Communion prayers (in reverse order), accompanied by the celebrant's washing of the chalice and his fingers. – KGW

[71] Cf. Sehling 1:6, *WA* 12:213 line 15ff., and *LW* 53:29 (paragraph VI and note 49 have the prayer in English). – KGW

[72] Sehling 3:69, Richter 1:327, and Müller p. 443 have *Sacramentum corporis tui* without any mention of *Perceptio*. The way it is in the Lutheran orders, it begins "Let not the sacrament of Your Body, Lord Jesus Christ . . . turn to our judgment and condemnation. . . ." The Roman version has "partaking" instead of "sacrament" and "my" instead of "our." – KGW

domine[73] and the *Quod ore sumpsimus*,[74] likewise deviating in nonessential linguistic nuances.[75] Many church orders expressly provided for an address or exhortation to the communicants prior to the Communion.[76] It is probably little known that the evangelical orders here follow a Catholic custom that arose in the Middle Ages and remained in practice, also in Catholic territory, into the late sixteenth century, from which we still possess three pertinent formulas (from the ritual books of Mainz 1551, Salzburg 1557, and Trier 1574), but which then declined, supposedly under the "overwhelming influence of the *Rituale Romanum*."[77] In place of the *Confiteor* before Communion, some church orders had a German formula for the public or general confession and absolution.[78] Usually a psalm, a portion of a psalm, or a German hymn was found at this point instead of the Communion verse and was thoroughly in line

---

[73] Cf. Sehling 1:6, *WA* 12:213 line 23f., and *LW* 53:29 (paragraph VII and note 53 have most of the prayer in English). – KGW

[74] Cf. Sehling 1:6, *WA* 12:213 line 23, and *LW* 53:29 (paragraph VII and note 52 have the prayer in English). – KGW

[75] Sehling 3:69f. and 101. In this regard, incidentally, both of these church orders, which were meant for the whole Electoral Mark and Old Mark regions, were more true to tradition than the proverbial highly traditional order of ceremonies for the Berlin cathedral chapter, which, however, mirrors the richness of late medieval liturgical forms in another area, for example in its rules for the daily office prayers, processions, and saints' days in the church year; Nikolaus Müller, "Zur Geschichte des Gottesdienstes der Domkirche zu Berlin in den Jahren 1540–1598." *Jahrbuch für brandenburgische Kirchengeschichte* 2/3 (1906): 337–551, especially 440–445. [The Roman Missal was standardized in 1570 as a result of the Council of Trent (hence the "Tridentine Mass"), but, aside from heavy use of abbreviations, earlier editions of these prayers differ only slightly from the Tridentine version.]

[76] Cf. Balthasar Fischer's collection of the oldest evangelical formulas in "Die Predigt vor der Kommunionspendung. Eine Skizze ihrer Geschichte im Abendland," in *Verkündigung und Glaube. Festgabe für Franz X. Arnold* (ed. by Theodor Filthaut and Joseph Andreas Jungmann, Freiburg: Herder, 1958), 329, note 30 [I was unable to obtain this essay, but find that it is supposed to be on pp. 223–237, thus this should probably be "229"]. As one example among many, I name the three *formulae exhortationis* in the 1564 Lüneburg church order, Sehling 6/1:546ff.

[77] Fischer (previous note), 232, 236f.: a copy of the Trier formula.

[78] For example Wolfenbüttel 1569, Sehling 6/1:144f., with an attached exhortation.

with the sense of the Roman missal. A collect or thanksgiving is consistently found at the point of the post-Communion, followed by a blessing based on Numbers 6:24.

By means of an exact comparison with supposed or certain models in his articles on Luther's liturgical reforms (1910), which dealt with a more narrowly defined subject, namely the Litany, collects, and versicles, Paul Drews ascertained that Luther reached with force "into the treasure of the Catholic liturgy" and took from it what appeared useful for his purposes; that, where it seemed expedient, he critically, freely, and easily transformed his models, but in part also remained very true to them.[79] If this is valid for the German liturgy, then it is even more valid for the Latin forms of the evangelical service.[80] Following Luther's example, the authors of the evangelical service orders reached back to the Latin missals, etc.; from these they not only took over what was desirable from or did not appear offensive to evangelical viewpoints, but apparently also stuck to the traditional form for the structure. Based on visitor reports from the great territorial church visitation 1579–83, isolated old missals, antiphonaries, and breviaries were found alongside writings of the Reformation in evangelical parish libraries in the Upper Palatinate.[81] The evangelical service orders from Nürnberg and Amberg demonstrably went back to late medieval liturgical works in great measure.[82] In Frankfurt an der Oder, pre-Reformation missals were still found in use at the end of the sixteenth century.[83] One even gets the impression that, in the course of the territorial consolidation of its churches, Lutheranism—as if under the influence of the Interim[84] on

---

[79] Drews, 61f., 106f.

[80] Cf. for example Drews, 42ff. on the evangelical Litany in Latin.

[81] Götz, *Wirren*, 40ff. [See also Katharina Frieb, *Kirchenvisitation und Kommunikation: die Akten zu den Visitationen in der Kuroberpfalz unter Ludwig VI. (1576–1583)*. München: Beck, 2006.]

[82] Ramge, 87.

[83] Heinrich Grimm, "Die liturgischen Drucke der Diözese Lebus," *Wichmann-Jahrbuch für die Diözese Berlin* 9/10 (1956), 51.

[84] The Interim refers to imperial decrees following the emperor's defeat of the Schmalkaldic League. Lutherans were forced to accept certain Roman Catholic doctrines and practices while being granted some concessions until a council could meet. The Augsburg Interim was decreed in May 1548, but discontent among Lutherans gave rise to modifications, known as the Leipzig Interim of December 1548. An English translation of these is in

the one hand, as a reaction to fanaticism and Calvinism on the other hand—referred back to the liturgical tradition of the Middle Ages more rigorously and consciously than during the stormy and productive first years of the Reformation, in which liturgical form was "left to the discretion of the individual liturgist."[85]

Essentially the same principles applied for the form of Matins and Vespers as for the Mass. It kept its structure and in particular several old components continued alongside reshaped parts. Matins was held in Latin on Sundays and on all or on designated weekdays in larger cities; an early sermon was commonly connected with it. Matins began with one to three Latin psalms, upon which followed, on Sundays and festivals, the antiphon for the Sunday or feast (*antiphona de dominica vel festo*), the reading of the Epistle in Latin or German, and the Te Deum. Later on Sundays and festivals a psalm (alternating weekly between German and Latin) and the Benedicamus [*Benedicamus Domino* = Let us bless the Lord] were sung, upon which the "priest" (parson) or deacon concluded with a collect. Finally came the sermon, marked specifically by bell tolls. One to two Latin psalms sufficed for the entrance on weekdays, after which a German psalm and the sermon were provided for; the sermon was concluded with a short psalm, again in German, and a collect. On certain weekdays, usually Wednesdays and Fridays, the Litany was provided for in village and city churches as a responsive prayer between the clergyman and the congregation. In cities, schoolboys sang the Latin psalms from the chancel.[86]

For Vespers, several versions developed according to purpose, place, and time, while maintaining the same basic structure. It had its appointed spot on Sundays and festivals, as well as on the days preceding those, i.e. regularly on Saturday. In the country it was held in German; in cities, insofar as it was connected with the Sunday

---

Sources and Contexts of the Book of Concord, ed. by Robert Kolb and James A. Nestingen (Minneapolis: Fortress Press, 2001), 144–196. – KGW

[85] Schmidt, 57, draws attention to the fact that "the multiplicity that had grown from this deregulation" troubled Luther already in 1526 and caused him to think of the "offensive confusion" it brought in its wake. [Cf. Luther's Preface to "The German Mass" in *LW* 53:61, *WA* 19:72 line 14f.]

[86] The provisions described here are in the important 1564 Lüneburg and 1569 Wolfenbüttel church orders, Sehling 6/1:141f., 153f., 541f., 551f., more in Graff 1:111f., 118f., especially 206–221; Ramge, 108.

catechesis for children, likewise in German. In this case it consisted of a German psalm, a German hymn, the German Magnificat, *Benedicamus Domino,* and a collect. On Sundays this liturgy was abbreviated for the sake of the catechesis, insofar as this was connected with the children's sermon.[87] —In the cities of Lower Saxony, the Sunday and festival solemn Vespers began as a separate service after the catechesis, at 2:00, with one to two Latin psalms, a reading, the Ten Commandments, the Creed, and the Our Father in German; the accompanying sermon on the Sunday Epistle introduced a hymn for the day or season (*de tempore*), sung alternatively in German or Latin; the conclusion was formed by the Magnificat with *Benedicamus Domino,* likewise sung alternatively in German or Latin, and a collect. Aside from the sermon, which was omitted on this day, the Saturday Vespers proceeded the same way.[88] The Amberg church order of 1583, which depended on the Nürnberg church order, provided for a Vespers that was to be structured about the same way for all weekdays and inserted catechism recitation after the reading for Sundays and festivals: Two boys recited the catechism questions and answers aloud from the chancel. In addition to this, a part of the Maundy Thursday Matins from the Roman breviary was prayed every Thursday during Vespers in Amberg and Nürnberg in remembrance of Christ's anguish on the Mount of Olives.[89]

C. INDIVIDUAL PARTS OF THE MASS

In addition to these reports concerning the continued existence of service forms of the Mass, Matins, and Vespers we will still look at a few notes on various details regarding either the form or the conduct of the service. In matters of the form of the Mass, we will first briefly note a few things concerning the place of the Creed in the structure of the Mass and the treatment of the preface, elevation, and Communion portion.

The Creed—the first four words of which, by the way, also the evangelical clergyman intoned ("I believe in one God" is four words in Latin, *Credo in unum Deum*) and then the choir took up and

---

[87] Thus Lüneburg 1564 and Wolfenbüttel 1569, Sehling 6/1:553f., 156.
[88] The church orders from Lower Saxony just mentioned and, almost in complete agreement with them, the 1574 Schwarzburg church order, Sehling 2:132f., with the reading of the (probably Sunday) Gospel on Saturday.
[89] Ramge, 91ff.

continued with "the Father Almighty" (*Patrem omnipotentem*)—by no means definitively occupied the place after the sermon up until the Reformation. Most Lutheran church orders had the sermon follow the Creed; however, not all. Graff lists a scant dozen examples of evangelical service orders in which the sermon preceded the Creed just as in the modern Roman missal. Also, however, it was occasionally spoken, as in Liegnitz, directly prior to receiving the Lord's Supper and after the exhortation.[90] But also in Catholic services of the sixteenth and seventeenth centuries the Creed was occasionally prayed or sung before the sermon. According to my understanding of a study by Balthasar Fischer, this was a widespread medieval custom, which has remained to the present in some places, such as the Bishopric of Trier.[91] The post-Tridentine Catholic Hildesheim hymnal from 1625 likewise prescribed for the Mass the order of Gospel, Creed, sermon, offertory.[92] It may perhaps be mentioned in this context that four boys had to genuflect at the altar in the castle church of Mansfeld during the words "and became man" (*Et incarnatus est*) in order to defend against the Flacian error.[93]

As regards the preface, it was treated very differently, insofar as it was not omitted altogether.[94] Some orders used it in monologue rather than dialogue form, as the 1525 Bremen church order or the

---

[90] Graff 1:163.

[91] Balthasar Fischer, "Ein Sonntagshochamt vor 400 Jahren," *Trierer theologische Zeitschrift* 66 (1957), 168ff. (with a description of a Christmas High Mass in the little town of Wittlich by Bishop Nicolas [Psaume/Psalmaeus] of Verdun in 1563, in his diary on the Council of Trent, *Diarium et Medulla Votorum Patrum Concilii Tridentini* II, 880).

[92] Graff 1:269f.

[93] Graff 1:164. Also according to the 1573 Hoya church order, three boys were to genuflect at the altar during the *Et incarnatus est*, Richter 2:353, cited according to Fendt, 343 (see note 101 below). [The Flacian error refers to the teaching of Matthias Flacius that original sin is not a quality (*accidens*) of human nature, but its essence (*substantia*), which he expressed in the 1560 Weimar Disputation in opposition to the errors of Victorin Strigel concerning original sin and the freedom of man's will. The Flacian error was rejected in 1577 in Article 1 of the Formula of Concord (Solid Declaration 1, 26ff.), along with other errors concerning original sin, while the errors concerning free will were rejected in Article 2.]

[94] As it was omitted by Luther, Graff 1:186; the 1568 church order for Prussia says that it was disposed of and should be left out, Sehling 4:81.

evangelical Mass from Kantz.[95] Sometimes it appears only as a daily preface (*praefatio quotidiana*),[96] sometimes in the various forms of the Roman missal for high feasts and Sundays after Pentecost, partly in German, partly in Latin;[97] partly elective,[98] partly obligatory;[99] often only on high feasts.[100] The Minden church order of 1530, in contrast, seems to have had few parallels with its unique connection of preface and consecration: First of all it was not common to have the formula for the Easter preface used here in the daily service; but it may perhaps have been even more unusual for the preface to be divided. It was sung until ". . . is raised and has brought us life again." Then followed the Words of Institution, the consecration, and the elevation. After "This do in remembrance of Me," the preface picked up again with "Therefore we sing with all angels" and flowed into the choral singing of the Sanctus and the Benedictus.[101] It eludes my knowledge whether or not medieval models existed for that.

The freedom of liturgical form at the beginning of the Reformation brought with it variations not only in the consecration

---

[95] Schmidt, 73.

[96] Schmidt, 73.

[97] The 1569 Wolfenbüttel church order, Sehling 6/1:180ff.

[98] Mecklenburg 1552, Sehling 5:199; Wolfenbüttel 1542, and the city of Braunschweig 1528, Sehling 6/1:59 and 443: to be used where advanced schoolboys are present.

[99] Braunschweig 1657 and 1709, Graff 1:186.

[100] Wolfenbüttel 1569, Sehling 6/1:180; Schwarzburg 1574, Sehling 2:133.

[101] The 1530 Minden church order has recently been published by Martin Krieg in: *Jahrbuch des Vereins für westfälische Kirchengeschichte* 43 (1950); the text of the preface is found there on 104f. Division of the preface by insertion of the consecration words is also found in the following church orders: Liegnitz 1535, Sehling 3:439; "Then one shall sing the preface, in which is enclosed the Lord's words concerning His Supper, followed by the Sanctus, *Discubuit* or *Homo quidam fecit*," Nördlingen 1549; Christian Geyer, *Die Nördlinger evangelischen Kirchenordnungen des XVI. Jahrhunderts* (München: Beck, 1896), 40ff.: The preface, "*Dominus vobiscum . . .*" until "*per Christum Dominum nostrum*"; the Words of Institution; the Sanctus. Cited according to Fendt, 310; Sweden 1576: The Christmas preface, "*Dominus vobiscum . . .*" until "*in invisibilium amorem rapiamur*"; the Words of Institution; the elevation; "*Et ideo cum angelis et archangelis* etc.; Pierre Le Brun, *Explication de la Messe* (Paris, 1726), IV, 162ff., cited according to Fendt, 313.

words, but also in the distribution formulas.[102] It may be mentioned all the same that, of the five distribution formulas that eventually established themselves, at least one, and indeed the shortest, had come from the Roman Mass,[103] and that although the *Verba Testamenti* of evangelical masses differed among themselves, all were still reminiscent of the version in the *Missale Romanum*.[104]

Within the evangelical Mass, perhaps the elevation of bread and wine directly following the consecration of the elements provided the strongest visible reminder of Catholic custom. Luther regarded it as an adiaphoron and simply retained it in Wittenberg at first.[105] Later he advocated its omission.[106] Thus for both, the use as well as the omission, one could henceforth appeal to Luther. Indeed, numerous church orders prohibited it; for this they appealed, such as the influential 1552 Mecklenburg church order, to "good and important reasons" and also gladly brought into relief that they thereby followed the example of other churches, which had likewise abrogated it.[107] The number of orders that either left the elevation as an option,[108] or

---

[102] From the 1598 advisory opinion of Brandenburg theologians, Müller, 529, we see that some of the prayers of the Canon of the Mass were whispered between the Sanctus and the consecration during the celebration of the Mass in the Berlin cathedral chapter. The opinion advises that the "words, which they call preparatory or quiet murmur, be abandoned" to guard against papistical superstition, and "to retain only the usual recitation of Christ's words."

[103] The body (the blood) of Jesus Christ preserve you unto eternal life. Amen! Graff 1:197ff.

[104] Schmidt, 75ff.; also his remark on 77: "With this an event is repeated in the Reformation that is known to the history of the liturgy already from earlier epochs: The oldest versions of the *Verba Testamenti* depart from the biblical text with unrestrained freedom, only later reforms seek alignment again."

[105] Sehling 1:6, 16, and 704f.: 1523 (*Formula Missae*), 1526 (*Deutsche Messe*), and the 1533 Wittenberg church order, respectively. – KGW

[106] Sehling 1:203: Wittenberg 1542.

[107] Sehling 5:199: Mecklenburg 1552.

[108] Sehling 1:403: Albertine Saxony. [Zeeden gives an incorrect page number here. Page 403 is in Elector August's 1580 order, where the elevation, if it were to be mentioned, should be found on p. 369, but it is neither there, nor on p. 403. He probably had in mind the 1545 Celle church order, Sehling 1:301.]

planned it for high feast days,[109] or strictly mandated it,[110] however, does not appear to be very much less. It survived very tenaciously in the entire territory of Electoral Brandenburg, from the Old Mark at the border of Lower Saxony to the New Mark at the Polish border. Against the will of the leading Reformation theologian Georg Buchholzer, Elector Joachim II enforced its retention in 1540. The corresponding instructions in the 1540 and 1572 church orders went back to the formulation of the Brandenburg Catholic missal from 1516. When Joachim's grandson Joachim Friedrich set out to purge the Mark's church liturgy in 1598 along with his theological advisors, neither the elector nor his churchmen dared to make too great a change in this point, although they regarded it as necessary. His cousin, Margrave Georg Friedrich of Ansbach, at the same time Regent of Prussia, whom he approached for advice, likewise recommended to him caution: The elevation is, this he wrote to him quite clearly, a papal abuse and therefore worthy of abrogation. Nevertheless, for Mark Brandenburg (where this "abuse" was so deeply rooted) he suggested proceeding with the greatest caution. He recommended to him "not to rush into sudden abrogation of the elevation or ostension,[111] but to acquiesce a little for now, until some point in the future when the parishioners have been better instructed from God's Word, and then probably gradually or even readily want to omit and abrogate it themselves."[112] In the course of doctrinal quarrels among Protestants, Elector Joachim II had instituted the ostension—to which Margrave Georg Friedrich alluded on this

---

[109] As Luther himself in the German Mass (1526) and in the 1533 Wittenberg church order.

[110] Cf. the compilation by Ernst Walter Zeeden, "Grundlagen und Wege der Konfessionsbildung," *Historische Zeitschrift* 185 (1958), 279 note 2.

[111] Ostension here refers to the showing of the Sacrament during the service, in connection with the elevation, rather than the Roman Catholic practice of keeping the Sacrament in a monstrance (ostensory) for adoration at other times. For more details concerning elevation and ostension in Brandenburg at this time, see Bodo Nischan, *Prince, People, and Confession: The Second Reformation in Brandenburg* (Philadelphia: University of Pennsylvania Press, 1994). Müller notes that the ostension was known only in the Berlin cathedral and in Frankfurt an der Oder in 1598 (p. 459, 530), and that it was probably abolished the same year in the Berlin cathedral and was abolished in Frankfurt an der Oder in 1600 (p. 460). – KGW

[112] Müller, 456f.

occasion and against which the electoral theologians less mildly advised intervening—as a sign of Evangelical orthodoxy in matters pertaining to the understanding of the Lord's Supper. He boasted in his testament (1563) of having "changed the elevation into the ostension" in opposition to the fanatic Paul Eber and "to the glory of God, as it was and still is preserved in the Greek Mass." Thereafter Andreas Musculus introduced it also in Frankfurt an der Oder. According to a statement of the 1598 Brandenburg theologians' advisory opinion, the ostension consisted of this: After the consecration, the priest "turns to the people and says before the distribution, 'Behold, dear Christians, this is the true body of our Lord Jesus Christ' etc. Likewise, 'Behold, dear Christians, this is the true blood,' etc." The congregation reacted to this in a manner still current among Catholics today, by which, of course, the advisors from 1598 were not very pleased, namely, "As soon as the simpleminded hear this, especially among the women, they beat their chest, or raise their hands, or act some other way, showing plenty traces of superstition."[113] Behind this stood the same sacramental realism, so it seems, which came to expression in the regulations concerning the careful handling of the elements of the Supper, which are still to be mentioned below.[114] The fact that pre-Reformation Catholic conceptions about Christ's presence in the Sacrament of the Altar carried on in such rites apparently cannot be entirely dismissed. That was also the opinion of the theological advisors. They therefore recommended abrogating this rite, as it gave occasion for the Brandenburgers to be attributed all kinds of abhorrent errors like *inclusio localis* (local inclusion) and *impanatio artolatria*,[115] and to claim that they affirmed such a presence of Christ's body and blood in bread and wine. That, being beyond the true institution and right use, would deviate from the true Lutheran creed and offend against it.[116]

---

[113] Müller, 457ff., 530.

[114] See the paragraph following note 125 below.

[115] It is unclear why Zeeden has these two nouns together in this fashion, but the meaning is likely: adoration of the consecrated bread resulting from the view of impanation (that Christ assumed the bread in the same way as He assumed the flesh in the Incarnation). – KGW

[116] Müller, 530.

From the very beginning the evangelical church orders showed a strong reservation regarding self-communion of the clergyman during the Mass and mostly rejected it.[117] The logical consequence of this is that the parts of the liturgy from the preface up to Communion, thus also the consecration, were only to be included if communicants were present. That in turn resulted in the formation of two service types: the service without and the service with communicants. Since participation in Communion was generally very low, it happened that the service without communicants strongly grew in significance. The pronounced awareness of sins and the high regard for the mystery of the Sacrament of the Altar had already greatly reduced reception of Communion in the high and late Middle Ages. The evangelical church orders stood in this line of tradition.[118] From this they drew the liturgical consequence and shortened the service: If there was no sermon, it concluded after the Gospel reading with a hymn, a collect, and the blessing. If there had been a sermon, the conclusion became a little more substantial in that, aside from the collect, they prayed either the Litany, or Simeon's canticle (Luke 2:29–32), or the Te Deum laudamus.[119] Here also one could refer to late medieval practice: Simeon's canticle was often prayed in the same place also in the pre-Reformation Catholic period;[120] and prior to the Reformation it was also widespread for people to leave the church after the sermon, or at least after the consecration.[121] Thus when the evangelical church orders drastically abbreviated the service without communicants, they accommodated here in what may perhaps only be an older practice. Theologically the thought was that the Mass without communicants, or the "private Mass" (*Winkelmesse*), was an abomination and reprehensible. It was that thought which came into play here and which Luther repeatedly addressed, for example in his

---

[117] As indicated later in this paragraph, Zeeden is referring to the private Mass, when a priest communed himself in the absence of any other communicants. – KGW

[118] Schmidt, 81f.

[119] As in the 1583 Lutheran church order of Amberg, Ramge, 106.

[120] Josef A. Jungmann, *Missarum Sollemnia* (4th ed., Vienna: Herder, 1958) vol. 2, p. 481, 501f., 504; thanks for the reference are due to Schmidt, 82f.

[121] Balthasar Fischer, "Ein Sonntagshochamt vor 400 Jahren," see note 91 above.

work *"Formula Missae,"*[122] which gave direction for structuring the evangelical service. In Protestantism, the daily Mass of pre-Reformation times effectively fell victim to this verdict on the private Mass. This was not always welcomed. Even such a resolutely Lutheran ruler as Margrave Georg of Ansbach pondered if it might not be good to reintroduce the old practice of the Mass with self-communion of the priest, so that the Communion portion of the Mass would not totally slip from the memory of the communicants on account of its absence. He of course desisted when Luther advised him in a letter to distance himself from such things.[123] The Berlin cathedral chapter service order offered an interesting example for rescuing the daily Mass: It prescribed that every day a chapter member had to commune and—by providing this one obligatory communicant for the weekday High Mass, which was to be celebrated in full liturgical splendor according to the will of the evangelical inspirator of the chapter order, Elector Joachim II—formally eliminated the character of the private Mass. This attempt at circumvention lasted until about 1600. In a still extant opinion from 1598, the theological advisors of Elector Joachim Friedrich (1598–

---

[122] Cf. "An Order of Mass and Communion for the Church at Wittenberg" in *LW* 53:15–40. See also, for example, Article 24 of the Augsburg Confession and its Apology, Part 2 Article 2 of the Smalcald Articles, "Abomination of the Secret Mass" (*LW* 36:307–328), and "Private Mass and the Consecration of Priests" (*LW* 38:139–214). – KGW

[123] Schmidt, 82; the absence of communicants set in motion the downfall of the Lutheran Sunday Mass in Schleswig-Holstein. Feddersen, 449. [Margrave Georg had expressed his desire to reinstate the private Mass in 1530. That same year at least three theologians wrote during the Diet of Augsburg to oppose such a move: Philipp Melanchthon wrote a letter to the margrave to dissuade him from this (July 30?, German translation in vol. 1, pp. 248–251 of *Philipp Melanchthon's Werke*, ed. by Friedrich A. Koethe, Leipzig: Brockhaus, 1829), in September Justus Jonas wrote an opinion opposing it (*Bedenken des Dr. J. Jonas betr. Wiederherstellung der Privatmessen*, included in the *Ernestinisches Gesamtarchiv* for the 1530 Diet of Augsburg, vol. 4, fol. 68–71), and Johann Brenz likewise wrote a brief opinion (cf. vol. 1, pp. 244f. in *Johann Brenz*, ed. by Julius Hartmann and Karl Jäger, Hamburg: Perthes, 1840). Apparently Margrave Georg was not convinced right away, as Luther's letter is dated Sept. 14, 1531. The margrave's 1533 church order (Brandenburg-Nürnberg), however, clearly states that Mass should no longer be held unless there are people present who desire to receive the Holy Sacrament (Richter 1:201).]

1608) vigorously complained that this abuse was still happening at the cathedral.[124] Concerning the self-communion of the clergyman holding the service, we can also indirectly verify its decline from this complaint. The Merseburg synodical instruction of 1544 and 1545, which was authored by the highly conservative evangelical Bishop Georg, Prince of Anhalt, himself, whose liturgical stance was close to that of the elector of Brandenburg, contained the direction that "also the priests who distribute the venerable Sacrament ought not to abstain from partaking of the same without a particular reason, as some do with not a little offense to the people."[125]

Naturally the numerous regulations concerning Communion distribution, which consistently occurred under both kinds, also inadvertently contained much about how the Sacrament was understood. More than once what stood behind them was a realistic conception that came rather close to the Catholic conceptions. This is apparent above all in the meticulous care with which the elements were handled, or should have been. The Merseburg synodical instruction prescribed: "And when something remains of the hosts or in the chalice, it should not be reserved (1545: set aside or poured out), but should be completely consumed by the priest or communicants who partook of the sacramental meal."[126] The same concern is voiced by the 1569 Pomeranian agenda, which obligated the clergyman to do the following when communing the sick: If the person was not able to keep the host in his mouth, he was to take it back and give an account of this to the superintendent. Then "the clergyman was obligated to bring the interrupted action to conclusion by consecrating more bread and using it with the already consecrated

---

[124] The text of this advisory opinion is in Müller, 526ff., the key passage being on p. 529: "First, in the administration of the holy Sacrament of the Altar, the practice up till now is supposed to have been that the HoMissarius [celebrant of the High Mass], as he is called when Mass is held, was always obligated to commune, and then the Vicarius who read the Gospel on Sunday, on Thursday the one who read the Epistle, and then one after another as determined by the order. This shows how such takes place more from custom than from pious devotion, and this results in quite a compulsion, such that many, on account of the order, had to do against their will—yes, with express indignation—that which they would forbear if it were voluntary. . . ."
[125] Sehling 2:18.
[126] Sehling 2:18.

wine."[127] In Weiden in the Upper Palatinate, the officiating clergyman communed every Sunday in order that, as he said on the occasion of the 1579–83 visitation, nothing of the Supper would be left over.[128] In Nittenau in the Upper Palatinate, the Lutheran parson set great value on the use of the houseling cloth,[129] "since otherwise the host would be blown away from him by people's breathing," or taken so clumsily by people that it fell to the floor. To the surly reaction of the Calvinistic visitors that these were coarse jokes, with which he should "not affirm the people in their coarseness," the parson stated for the record that, on the contrary, this is a "holy matter" (*res sacra*).[130] And during the same 1574 visitation, when a parson from Pittersberg in the Upper Palatinate, likewise a Lutheran, was examined on his understanding of the Sacrament and confessed that he firmly believes "that a consecration actually takes place and the bread is essentially (*essentialiter*) the body of Christ,"[131] the visitors took him to mean he believed in "papistic transubstantiation."[132] On the background of such conceptions, which can be attested in various places for central, northern, and southern Germany between 1540 and 1580, what the 1540 Brandenburg church order prescribed concerning sick calls no longer sounds so peculiar. Since this is also not entirely without interest for cultural history, it shall briefly be restated: Thereafter, as a rule, the Sacrament should be consecrated for the sick call in an ordinary service and be kept on the altar. At the appropriate time, it should then be carried into the house of the sick person "with due reverence"; that is, the sacristan had to precede the parson, who wore a surplice,[133] with a lamp while ringing a little bell. Also for sudden sick calls, the consecration had to take place beforehand in the

---

[127] Plantiko, 139; briefer and less precise is Hellmuth Heyden, *Kirchengeschichte Pommerns* vol. 2, p. 60 (2nd ed., Köln: R. Müller, 1957); Sehling 4 prints only excerpts from the 1569 agenda and omits the chapter on communing the sick.

[128] Götz, *Wirren*, 51.

[129] Typically a white linen cloth held in front of communicants to catch any crumbs that might fall from the host, thereby preventing them from touching the floor. – KGW

[130] Götz, *Einf.*, 137.

[131] According to the Lutheran interpretation, no transformation is effected, rather the body of Christ is in, with, and under the bread.

[132] Götz, *Einf.*, 138.

[133] *Chorrock*, see notes 137 and 144 below. – KGW

church. That applied to cities. In villages, however, the consecration should not occur until in the house. Why? Because—with the excessive impracticable roadway conditions in the country, which often compelled the parson to go over rotten planks, and to climb over hedges and fences, or to ride far across the country—there was too much "danger" for the consecrated Sacrament—aside from other complications, such as this: With the delay resulting from the great distances, the sick person might no longer be able to partake of the consecrated host.[134] The detail of this reason not only inadvertently gives us a clear picture of the travel conditions of a bygone time, which of course also belong to the rudimentary living conditions of the corresponding historical epoch, but also lets shimmer through how realistic the understanding of the Sacrament still was after the first decades of the Reformation. In the present case this was true in Electoral Brandenburg; by all appearances, however, not just there.[135]

II. CONCERNING THE APPEARANCE
AND IMPLEMENTATION OF THE SERVICE

As for the appearance and implementation of the service, Lutheranism in central and northern Germany retained the liturgical colors, vestments, and vessels of the ancient church. Further, the evangelical Mass took over a good part of the wealth of the Catholic liturgy's actions; it also took over the chanting of the priest and

---

[134] Sehling 3:77–80.

[135] The 1540 order for the chapter service in Stendal, Sehling 3:308: Although the reformer Conrad Cordatus was inducted into the recently vacated position of chapter dean with the title of vice-dean, he was denied jurisdiction over the canons, who, together with the chapter vicars, had choir duty imposed on them. Moreover, Cordatus had to see to it that, whenever people wanted to commune on Sundays or weekdays, "the Mass would always be held." To wit, it should be sung by the chapter choir with the same number of singers and in the same manner as previously, "and, in addition, be ministered by the vicars as previously." [Choir duty (*Chordienst*) meant singing the canonically regulated prayer hours (choir offices) in the choir (chancel).]

The detailed interpretation of the highly conservative 1540 Brandenburg church order was recently published by Hans Bernard Klaus, *Missa. Untersuchungen zur Gestalt der evangelischen Messe im 16. Jahrhundert in Berlin-Brandenburg* (Göttingen: Vandenhoeck & Ruprecht, 1952).

people, and principally also the Latin language, even if not to the extent of its use in the pre-Reformation Church. Alongside the liturgical actions, the church furnishings and fixtures were also retained to a certain degree, from the baptismal font and pictures to the banners and procession poles.

A. LITURGICAL VESTMENTS AND OBJECTS FOR THE SERVICE

Lutherans continued to use the five ancient liturgical colors as well as the liturgical vestments in the service and for sacramental acts; this usage lasted amazingly long, partly up to the brink of the nineteenth century. Insofar as Calvinism hadn't discredited these earlier,[136] they mostly disappeared first under the influence of the Enlightenment in the late eighteenth century. Apparently the Interim also contributed to usage of the chasuble and surplice[137] becoming more firmly established. But also independently from this, liturgical vestments

---

[136] Such as with Anhalt's crossover to the Reformed confession at the end of the sixteenth century, Graff 1:107f., or in the highly conservative Berlin-Brandenburg Electorate since the close of the seventeenth century, as seen in the "Political Testament" of Friedrich Wilhelm the Great Elector [1667]: "and, God be praised, the Brandenburg Electorate and Pomerania have been totally freed from gross papal abominations and idolatry, aside from what the Lutherans have retained in their churches from the papacy in the way of ceremonies, which of course you should endeavor to abolish if that can be done in an agreeable manner," Vol. 1, p. 44 of *Die politischen Testamente der Hohenzollern nebst ergänzenden Aktenstücken*, ed. by Georg Küntzel and Martin Hass (Leipzig; Berlin: B. G. Teubner, 1911).

[137] *Chorrock* will always be translated here as "surplice," even though *Chorhemd* is translated likewise. Arthur Carl Piepkorn notes: "The two terms are interchangeable as designations for the white alb-like vestment. It should be noted that *Chorrock* has several meanings. During the sixteenth century it designated the white surplice exclusively." *The Survival of the Historic Vestments in the Lutheran Church after 1555.* (2nd ed., St. Louis: Concordia Seminary, 1958), p. 6, note 4. The use of *Chorhemd* for the surplices of the choir boys points to the fact that there were various forms of this garment, such as those of shorter sleeve and overall length, often worn by acolytes and choir members. Note 1 of Sehling 11:44 calls the *Chorrock* a *superpelliceum* and describes it as a white shirt-like garment reaching to the knees with broad sleeves that was worn for official acts outside of the Mass; it could be worn by the sexton, crucifer, and others. He points to other literature and asserts that equation of this garment with the alb is erroneous, but see note 144 below. – KGW

enjoyed the greatest favor in Lutheranism of northern and central Germany. How greatly Lutheranism changed back to the conservative line on this point can be inferred quite nicely from Walter Delius' reports on the 1555 visitation in the archiepiscopal-Magdeburg subdistrict (*Amt*) of Querfurt[138]: The visitation showed that only three parishes still had chasubles in use; after that, all churches in the county were required to use them again; the parsons whose chasubles had disappeared had to go to Querfurt Castle and there be given new vestments.[139] As far as lifespan goes, the ecclesiastical vestments remained in Weissenfels until 1588 and in Silesia until 1811. In Hamburg the celebrants wore an ornate chasuble during the Lord's Supper until 1785;[140] in Lusatia the choir boys wore surplices until 1850 (they wore these while holding the houseling cloths during Communion). Chasubles, which were regarded as a worthy ornament and therefore gladly retained, were also occasionally reinstated even in the later evangelical period. Thus they were used in 1740 in Silesia for consecrating new congregations; in 1659 they were reintroduced into Mecklenburg, in order thereby to serve a counterblow to the "libertinism and negligence of divine worship (*libertinismo und negligentia cultus divini*), which unfortunately are growing ever more prevalent from day to day."[141] The chasuble was, like the ceremonies, regarded as a symbol of the difference between Calvinism and as a criterion for pure Lutheranism,[142] just as conversely, wherever Calvinism gained access, it immediately insisted on abolishing the surplice and chasuble.[143] In the realm of the Saxon territories, the celebrant removed the chasuble over his head before the sermon, laid

---

[138] Here "*Amt*" designates an association of municipalities, an administrative unit below the level of a district (*Landkreis*). The subdistrict of Querfurt was politically bound with the Archbishopric of Magdeburg. – KGW

[139] Delius, 79ff.

[140] Per a friendly note to the author from Prof. H. Kellinghusen on July 28, 1958; according to Graff 1:107 this continued until 1788.

[141] Counterexample: Schleswig-Holstein, where, despite the order of the 1542 church order to use albs (*Alba*) and chasubles, the chasubles were not repaired when worn-out, and thereby fell out of use, in contrast to Denmark: Feddersen, 449f.

[142] Cf. for example the 1592 church order for the Margraviate of Lower Lusatia, Sehling 3:363.

[143] Numerous examples in Götz, *Einf.* 97, 132f.

it on the altar, preached in his alb,[144] and afterward put on the chasuble again. The same happened in Schleswig-Holstein; it was similar also in the Halberstadt territory. In Nürnberg, where, as elsewhere in southern Germany, not the chasuble, but only the surplice was retained, the celebrant took off the surplice before the sermon with the help of the sexton and put it on with him after the sermon to continue the service.[145]

Of the objects for the service with which pre-Reformation churches tended to be furnished, they kept altars, candles, pictures, and sculptures;[146] likewise baptismal fonts and basins, bells, procession poles and banners, as well as little bells, which were rung during the service as a signal, for example during the elevation.[147] Even the otherwise severely frowned upon monstrance remained in some churches, indeed even remarkably long in Stendal's Jacobi church.[148] Censers remained more widely spread. In fact, some places used incense more out of health concerns, for example to improve the air or to guard against the plague; sometimes even to warm the church a little during the cold season. At the same time, swinging the censer for liturgical purposes also remained in practice, for example in the

---

[144] *Alba*, "In ordinary reference alb and surplice were not carefully differentiated from each other. After the Reformation the assimilation rapidly became complete in the Church of Augsburg Confession and the names became quite interchangeable" (Arthur Carl Piepkorn, *The Survival of the Historic Vestments in the Lutheran Church after 1555*, 2nd ed., St. Louis: Concordia Seminary, 1958, p. 2). Differentiation did occur at times, though. Gunter Tietz notes that two church inventories in the electoral district of Saxony reported the acquisition of an alb and a surplice (*einer Albe und eines Chorrockes*), p. 122 of *Das Erscheinungsbild von Pfarrstand und Pfarrgemeinde des sächsischen Kurkreises im Spiegel der Visitationsberichte des 16. Jahrhunderts* (Dissertation phil., Tübingen, 1971). – KGW

[145] The reports on the presence and use of the chasuble, if not otherwise indicated, closely follow Graff 1:106f.; on Schleswig-Holstein, see Feddersen, 446f.

[146] On this point, however, various changes occurred; sometimes these things were strictly reduced to a minimum—Ottheinrich of the Palatinate even had the pictures totally removed—sometimes churches were left essentially with the furnishings there at the time of the change.

[147] Graff 1:100f.; Feddersen, 447f. note 29.

[148] Graff 1:100f.

Magdeburg cathedral before celebrating the Lord's Supper, or in the Duchy of Weimar during Christmas Matins.[149]

B. LATIN AS A CHURCH LANGUAGE

As for other things concerning the conduct of the service, Latin, the priest's and choir's chant for particular portions of the service, and an abundance of liturgical actions, particularly of the clergyman, but also of the people, remained on principle from the ancient church. Chanting of the Epistle and collects were, to be sure, sometimes also dispensed with, although it was normally provided for.[150] Whoever has a rusty voice, so it says in the 1591 church order from Goldstein in Upper Silesia, should leave out the singing and rather read the collects etc. slowly and clearly.[151] Aside from custom, various other reasons, practical as well as pedagogical, spoke in favor of retaining Latin in the service. No one took offense at Latin on principle, because it was regarded as an adiaphoron. Further, it was regarded as beneficial from didactic viewpoints; Luther himself and Bugenhagen vigorously stressed this—the latter, for example, in the 1528 church order for the city Braunschweig.[152] In Prussia, Latin was additionally viewed as apt on account of the many "non-Germans" there. Practical considerations also spoke in favor of remaining with Latin in matters of choral chant: Since at first the ancient church tones and melodies were adhered to, German translations of psalms, sequences, etc.

---

[149] Graff 1:102f.

[150] Graff 1:167.

[151] Sehling 3:479.

[152] They were interested in teaching not only liturgical Latin, but also classical Latin, and in preparing schoolboys well for service in the church as well as in society. Retention of Latin was important not only for worship and theological study, but also as a means for enriching the German nation and because of its role as a world language. The 1533 Wittenberg church order even says that schoolboys should not sing in German in services unless the people sing along (Sehling 1:703) and describes the Latin boy's school, in which the teachers were to strive to have the boys speak in Latin (706f.). See also, for example, "To the Councilmen of All Cities in Germany That They Establish and Maintain Christian Schools," (*LW* 45:356–360), "Instructions for the Visitors of Parish Pastors in Electoral Saxony," written by Melanchthon, but also containing Luther's thoughts (*LW* 40:307, 314–320, which also has a description of the Latin boy's school), and "The German Mass and Order of Service" (*LW* 53:62f., 69). – KGW

would have to fit the given notes and their rhythm. Such a setting of German texts to ancient melodies did not, however, always prove to be feasible. Thus the ancient church language understandably held out the longest in the kinds of services having the most choral chant, Matins and Vespers.[153] Latin hymns from the Middle Ages found entry into evangelical hymnals even into the eighteenth century. In other respects, the continued use of older service forms in Lutheranism can be traced not only to uncritical retention of what was customary; precisely some of the leaders of the Reformation fostered a conscious bond with tradition. In 1529 Melanchthon urged upon the parson in Coburg to change as little as possible in the service and to preserve the bond with the past; he therefore also implored him to retain some Latin components even in the village service.[154] In an advisory opinion on worship reform, the Saxon theologians gathered in Leipzig in 1544 expressed their desire to have Latin not totally disappear since the Old and New Testaments are written in Latin (!)[155]—which in other words could only mean that when they read Holy Scripture, they reached for the Vulgate. Just how much people were attached to the ancient church language, and just how much they regarded it as belonging to the service, is clear from numerous statements in the church orders. The Pomeranian church order of 1569 spoke of "old Christian, magnificent chants, especially sequences and responsories."[156] The Hamburg Articles of 1535, adopted by clergy from numerous cities of the Hanseatic League[157] at their convention in Hamburg as a kind of synodical treaty, not only decisively opposed the otherwise prevailing disdain for Latin by the

---

[153] Here one should also take into account that the schoolboys were to sing in Latin when the people were not present. The fact that weekday Matins and Vespers were primarily attended by schoolboys contributed to the continued use of Latin in those services. – KGW

[154] CR 1:991 [the year there is 1528]; quotations for continued fostering of Latin are in Graff 1:167, whom I follow here.

[155] Emil Sehling, Die Kirchengesetzgebung unter Moritz von Sachsen 1544–1549 und Georg von Anhalt (Leipzig: Deichert, 1899), 12. [Sehling's statement is somewhat different: With regard to ceremonies they did not want singing in Latin to be totally abolished. This desire was motivated by the fact that the Old and New Testaments are written in Latin and by the fear that otherwise knowledge of Latin would decrease even more.]

[156] Sehling 4:470.

[157] Hamburg, Bremen, Lübeck, Rostock, Stralsund, Lüneburg, Wismar.

mob, but also precisely represented the view that "it is necessary to use Latin in the church." And although the same articles conceded with respect to the people (*"ne suo exercitio careat populus"* [that the people may not be without exercise]) that it was allowable at times to insert German hymns in the service, that was conceived of more in the sense of a concession. The authors of the articles regarded translation into German of all sung texts of the liturgy as downright dangerous: For if German were sung exclusively, then religion would unavoidably suffer damage, and finally all dignity of the service would go to ruin.[158] As an addendum concerning the tenacious lifespan of the ancient church language in Lutheranism of northern Germany, it is noted that the high feast antiphons were sung in Latin in Hamburg until 1767,[159] and that some town council decrees from November and December of 1790 first led to the gradual abrogation of Latin from the service in Lübeck.[160]

C. LITURGICAL ACTIONS

As it stood with Latin, so also with an abundance of ulterior rites, actions, and customs: They were taken over from the pre-Reformation period and lived on in the Lutheran Church, altered more or less. Insofar as they did not contain anything decisively unevangelical, no offense was taken at them. Concerning what was and was not evangelically tolerable, however, opinions diverged and views differed from one another. Thus the selection and mixture of that which was preserved from the realm of actions, rites, and vessels differed according to region and territory, or at least differed in part.

Concerning the actions (kneeling, standing, making the sign of the cross, etc.), Luther had judged that, as mere acts, they are worthless; as the expression of a sincere inner mindset of worship and adoration of God, however, they are useful and promote devotion. The Lutheran church orders accentuated the latter and took over a range of actions; to put it more accurately, on this point they left much as it had been. That was true especially for the worship acts of

---

[158] Sehling 5:541f. *Nam si germanica [lingua] tantum canerentur [psalmi et cantica], fieri non posse, quin sensim vilesceret religio, ut tandem omnis decor ceremoniarum prorsus interiret.* [Bracketed additions by Zeeden.]

[159] Per a friendly note from Prof. H. Kellinghusen, Hamburg-Bergedorf, on July 28, 1958.

[160] Sehling 5:329.

the clergy at the altar, but to a certain extent also for the people's conduct in the church. From the Upper Palatinate, which crossed over to the Reformation early and steadfastly defended itself against the design of the Heidelberg electors to force Calvinism upon it, there are visitation reports from the outgoing sixteenth and early seventeenth century such as this: A parson got agitated about an old man taking a seat during the Gospel reading (1574); or because some people still reverently bowed before the only crucifix that had been left in the church of Auerbach.[161]

The liturgical and extra-liturgical use of the sign of the cross appears to have been judged and handled quite differently. A Brandenburg advisory opinion from 1598, on whose composition the later General Superintendent Pelargus admittedly partook and soon thereafter turned Calvinist, took unusually severe offense at the Berlin cathedral clergymen's custom—supposedly not common otherwise—of making a cross over the bread or host, "as if by virtue and power of the form of the cross (*virtute et vi crucis formatae*) the presence of Christ's body would be effected," and recommended abrogating this action.[162] In contrast, the sign of the cross over bread and wine made an especially strong appearance precisely in the seventeenth century, according to the sources referred to by Graff,[163] and was widespread at the distribution of the Sacrament.[164] The 1598 advisory opinion of Berlin theologians recommended "that the cross be made according to the ancient custom of the Church only once, when the benediction is spoken,"[165] and appealed to the "manner of other churches" for this. The Lutheran Amberg catechism from 1595, on the contrary, recommended making the sign of the cross also for private piety: "Mornings, when you get out of bed, ... Evenings, when you go to bed, you should bless yourself with the holy cross."[166] In Neumarkt

---

[161] Götz, *Einf.*, 133; *Wirren*, 233.

[162] Müller, 529; cf. also 455: Making the sign of the cross at the consecration of the blood was also practiced in the Mark, although it was not provided for in the church orders!

[163] Graff 1:193.

[164] Graff 1:200f.

[165] Müller, 529.

[166] Ramge, 93 [This was already in Martin Luther's Small Catechism (1529), in the section "How the head of the family should teach his household to bless themselves in the morning and evening."]; cf. also the 1570 Kurland church order: "In the houses therefore ... morning and evening prayer

the congregation was still "blessed with the sign of the cross" in 1596.[167]

Many church orders expressly prescribed kneeling at the consecration, such as Prussia 1568, Schleswig-Holstein 1637, Hohenlohe 1700, and Mecklenburg 1708. The Gotha order of 1645 added to this that even the dignitaries had to kneel (though in their stalls), and likewise the men. In Isny the pastor kneeled at the consecration.[168] It was still widely customary in the seventeenth century to genuflect or exercise other "*reverentia*" when the name of Jesus was spoken. Johann Valentin Andreae increased the actions in his utopia of the model Christian state, in the *respublica Christianopolitana* of 1619: The congregation there was to kneel, raise their hands, or beat their chest at the times appointed during the service.[169] Conversely the Reformed clergy and authorities, who did not much care for those kinds of things, took severe steps against them. In 1596 the county-court judge of Auerbach (Upper Palatinate) received instruction from his Calvinistic government to question women seen there kneeling before a cross.[170] And since in 1615 a Reformed parson in Holnstein in the Upper Palatinate ranted about genuflecting and removing one's hat (before the crucifix) being "nothing but the devil's work," we can conclude that Lutheranism had survived well there.[171] Only since the seventeenth century did the

---

should be held for everyone, especially the little children—and that without scorn for the sign of the holy cross—which without any superstition are signs of our faith and confession (*signa fidei et confessionis nostrae*), the Christian's banner and ensign. And on account of this, the sign of the holy cross at the Lord's Supper is called the shield of faith, the impenetrable wall of believers (*scutum fidei, inexpugnabilis murus credentium*) in the *Lives of the Fathers* (*vitae patrum*)." Sehling 5:91.

[167] Götz, *Wirren*, 237. [Neumarkt is in the Upper Palatinate.]

[168] Graff 1:192; in Schleswig-Holstein it was "often customary, and the visitors generally desired that the communicants kneel at the Words of Institution. In some places already the Lord's Prayer was listened to while kneeling." Feddersen, 447 note 28. [Hohenlohe County is in the northern tip of Württemberg. Isny is a little east of Lake Constance.]

[169] *Reipublicae Christianopolitanae descriptio* (Strassburg [Argentorati: Zetzner], 1619), 179ff. [trans. by Edward H. Thompson under the title *Christianopolis* (Dordrecht; Boston: Kluwer Academic Publishers, 1999)], cited from Graff 1:285.

[170] Götz, *Wirren*, 237.

[171] Götz, *Wirren*, 310.

Lutheran authorities increasingly weaken on this point. In 1655 the Leipzig Theology department recommended slowly putting an end to congregation members as well as midwives with baptismal candidates kneeling before the altar, likewise to people genuflecting whenever a clergyman walked by.[172]

Concerning the continuation of actions and use of liturgical vestments, ceremonies, and furnishings, it can still be mentioned that in 1736, King Friedrich Wilhelm I of Prussia, who was affiliated with Pietism, religiously zealous, and interested in the church, perhaps in executing the recommendations of his grandfather the Great Elector,[173] prohibited the following as "*Puppenwerk*" (as child's play or frivolous): candles on the altar, chasubles and surplices, the chanting of the clergyman at the altar and his facing the altar (instead of the people) as well as making the sign of the cross; he also forbade a cross to be carried in front of a funeral procession. It remained for the enlightened King Friedrich the Great, of all people, to lift this ban and thereby make room again for the ancient church ceremonies in the Lutheran Church in the kingdom of Prussia.[174]

III. SACRAMENTS AND OCCASIONAL FEES

In matters of priestly acts and administration of the sacraments the practice of the Lutheran churches differed little from the practice of the Catholic period, although a different theology stood behind it. Whoever wanted to commune had to go to confession beforehand. The clergy were required to be available for hearing confession and

---

[172] Graff 1:285; the department thought there was a certain danger in this of turning to the false faith in the Catholic way. From the standpoint of folklore, there is also an interesting note here regarding the rites for men *removing their hat*. On principle they kept it on in the church and took it off only briefly when entering (for a silent prayer). The next time the hat was removed was at the collect; it was put on again for the pericopes, and was removed only briefly when the names Jesus, Immanuel, Alpha and Omega, and the like were read. The 1614 Ratzeburg church order prescribed that when the catechism was read (by the sacristan), the men should stand, and should also remove their hat at the words on which the sermon was to be preached.

[173] See note 136 above.

[174] Friedrich Uhlhorn, *Geschichte der deutsch-lutherischen Kirche* (Leipzig: Dörffling & Franke, 1911) Vol. 2, p. 14; Graff 1:109 with information on special literature for particular parts of Prussia.

administering absolution on Saturday afternoons—and for people with infirmities, also early on Sundays. Although according to the dogmatic conviction that gradually prevailed in the course of the Reformation there was not an actual sacrament of penance,[175] private confession and absolution still remained in practice in the Lutheran Church for centuries. Only in the late seventeenth and eighteenth century was it supplanted by the general confession. As a rule, even the confessor's fee had to be paid then as before. And corresponding with the more precise pastoral bookkeeping, which set in with the Reformation and the Council of Trent, the clergyman was charged with filling out the confession register and reporting delinquents to higher authorities. Of the two sacraments recognized by Protestantism as sacraments in the full sense, only Communion or the Lord's Supper visibly departed from the traditional form of distribution by using the form of distribution under both kinds (*sub utraque specie*). The differences in the act of Baptism stood out much less and were hardly noticeable for the laity. The evangelical formulas and rites for Baptism remained at least partially the same as before. Aside from a small number of exceptions, Lutheranism retained the exorcism prayer at Baptism. Although evangelical theology denied a sacramental character to the other sacraments of the Catholic period, confirmation, ordination, marriage, and extreme unction, they at least remained in practice as acts in some way, although only very attenuated in some cases; the rites bound with them were of course dropped in great number, commensurate with the changed theology.

So far the general picture. Beyond this, many a traditional practice still lived on in isolation or localized in certain territories, cities, or countrysides. Some of these will also be mentioned in what follows. First, however, a few words about the number and definition of the sacraments.

In the Latin version of the Apology of the Augsburg Confession, a treatise that after all has been elevated to the status of an official confession of Lutheranism, Melanchthon expressed in no uncertain terms that these—as distinct from all sorts of ceremonies and outward signs established merely by men—belonged to the true and proper sacraments instituted by God: Baptism, the Lord's Supper, and the Absolution: "Therefore *Baptism*, the *Lord's Supper*, and *Absolution*, which is the Sacrament of Repentance, are truly Sacraments" (*vere*

---

[175] Cf., however, Melanchthon in the Apology in the following footnote.

igitur sunt sacramenta baptismus, coena Domini, absolutio, quae est sacramentum poenitentiae).[176] In contrast, Melanchthon numbered confirmation and unction among the ceremonies "that were received from the ancient Fathers, which even the Church has never regarded as necessary for salvation" [Apology XIII, 6]; and concerning marriage, which was undoubtedly instituted by God, he supposed that if it were to be numbered among the sacraments, "then the other offices and estates that also come from God's Word and command would also have to be called sacraments, such as authorities and magistrates" [Apology XIII, 15].[177] He thought differently, however, concerning consecration of priests. Surely, he said, we have no priests who bring sacrifices as in the old covenant; "But if ordination [Zeeden: priesthood] be understood as applying to the ministry of the Word, we are not unwilling to call ordination a sacrament": *Si autem*

---

[176] *BSLK*, 292: Apology XIII, 4 "On the Sacraments." [The translation here and for the following Latin excerpts are from *Concordia Triglotta* (ed. by Friedrich Bente, St. Louis: Concordia Publishing House, 1921), p. 309, 311.] The text continues: "For when we are baptized, when we eat the Lord's body, when we are absolved, our hearts must be firmly assured that God truly forgives us for Christ's sake." (*Certo enim debent statuere corda, cum baptizamur, cum vescimur corpore Domini, cum absolvimur, quod vere ignoscat nobis Deus propter Christum!*) This sentence, as well as the preceding "which is the sacrament of penitence" disappears in the German translation of the Apology by Justus Jonas, which actually appears to be out to weaken Melanchthon's statements on the sacramental character of absolution. [He did not drop the entire sentence, but did omit "which is the Sacrament of Repentance" and "when we are absolved" and moved the rest to just ahead of the Romans 10 quote in XIII, 5.] Cf. Apology XIII, 14 *BSLK*, 294 (left col. line 14): "Wherefore, if any one should wish to call it [matrimony] a sacrament, he ought still to distinguish it from those preceding ones, which are properly signs of the New Testament, and testimonies of grace and the remission of sins" (*Quare si quis volet [matrimonium] sacramentum vocare, discernere tamen a prioribus illis [sacramentis] debet, quae proprie sunt signa novi testamenti et sunt testimonia gratiae et remissionis peccatorum*) [the bracketed insertions are from Zeeden], translated by Jonas (right col. line 21) as: "therefore if someone wants to call it [marriage] a sacrament, we will not dispute greatly. Nevertheless it should be distinguished from the previous *two*, which are true signs and seals of the New Testament." This, though Melanchthon (*BSLK*, 292) had expressly spoken of *three*.

[177] *BSLK*, 293, 294. [Zeeden quotes the German, which differs only slightly from the Latin.]

ordo de ministerio verbi intelligatur, non gravatim vocaverimus ordinem sacramentum [Apology XIII, 11]. For the preaching office is instituted by God and has magnificent promises (Romans 1 and Isaiah 55). Taking into consideration these promises, it seemed unobjectionable to Melanchthon to call the laying on of hands (at ordination) a sacrament, that is, to see in it the actual sacramental act: "If ordination be understood in this way, neither will we refuse to call the imposition of hands a sacrament" (*Si ordo hoc modo intelligatur, neque impositionem manuum vocare sacramentum gravemur*) [Apology XIII, 12].[178] The further development of the ordination practice and its theological interpretation showed, in the words of one evangelical character, that "in this point" they remained rather firmly "under the spell of Roman views."[179] That pertained not merely to the practice of ordination, but also to the sacramental acts and acts related with them, as well as their liturgical structure in general.

To begin with Baptism: Here Luther himself had given a first example of strict conservatism in his Baptism booklet of 1523. Aside from very small cuts, it was a translation of baptismal rituals from Magdeburg and Brandenburg current in central Germany. This first Baptism booklet, which was criticized for its papistic ceremonies even by his closest friends and many fellow reformers,[180] included among other things the putting of salt in the baptismal candidate's mouth (*datio salis*), *exsufflatio* or breathing on the baptismal candidate, wiping the ears and nose with spittle, anointings, clothing the baptismal candidate with a white shirt, and presenting a candle; additionally there were the greater and lesser exorcisms.[181] This form of the baptismal ceremony, among others, passed into the 1540 church order of Electoral Brandenburg. Elector Joachim II, who had issued it, still held fast to the traditional forms even later, in contrast to Luther, and prescribed in his 1563 testament, for example, that the

---

[178] *BSLK*, 293f.

[179] Graff 1:386 according to Grützmacher, cf. further the remarks in Graff 1:386ff.

[180] Georg Merz and Otto Dietz in the notes on the Baptism booklet of 1526, Luther, *Ausgewählte Werke* III (3rd ed., München: Christian Kaiser, 1950) (Munich edition), 420.

[181] *WA* 12:38ff. [Cf. *LW* 53:95–103. The rite begins with the exsufflation and lesser exorcism, "Depart, you unclean spirit, and make room for the Holy Spirit."]

so-called greater exorcism was to be retained. It read: "I adjure you, unclean spirit, by the name of God the Father ✝ and the Son ✝ and the Holy Spirit ✝, to come out and depart from this servant of Jesus Christ, ___name___. Amen." This greater exorcism, which Luther originally included together with the lesser exorcism for Baptism, was still taken into the 1583 Amberg church order.[182] The inventory of the Berlin cathedral chapter in 1599 contained salt and chrism boxes, which gives ground to the assumption that the old baptismal ritual was in use there at least until about 1599.[183] Aside from that, more of the rites mentioned above probably fell with the cuts Luther made in the 1526 Baptism booklet (*datio salis, exsufflatio, Ephphatha* [Mark 7:34], anointings, candle, greater exorcism). Yet the *abrenuntiatio*, the renunciation of the devil, and the shorter version of the exorcism, "Depart, you unclean spirit, and make room for the Holy Spirit," among other things, remained.[184] Both persevered almost continuously in Lutheranism and were also so deep in the consciousness of the people that wherever these rites were touched— Calvinism sought to dispose of them on principle—, tough battles and disputes ensued to preserve them. While the Calvinistic clergy in the Upper Palatinate shot against the exorcism with the heaviest artillery and sought to discredit it as "magic that came from the pope" or, according to Olevian, as "idolatry, a perversion of God's Word, a humiliation . . . of Christ," even as a sin against the Holy Spirit,[185] the

---

[182] Ramge, 110. [This is the same greater exorcism as in the 1526 Baptism booklet. In the 1523 Baptism booklet, the greater exorcism is a little longer, preceded by two more adjurations, and followed by a prayer before the reading from Mark 10. Cf. *LW* 53:97f., 108. The introduction to the 1526 Baptism booklet in the *WA* notes (19:532) that this version was soon appended to the Small Catechism and spread widely as a result. Many church orders simply referred to this Baptism booklet for the rite and other rites used it as a model. The Book of Concord did not include the booklet, however, due to fears that southern Germans would take offense at the exorcism.]

[183] Müller, 465, 534.

[184] Baptism booklet etc. 1526, *WA* 19:531ff. [Cf. *LW* 53:106–109]. [This "shorter version" is the same lesser exorcism as in 1523, although without the exsufflation. The greater exorcism is still present, but shorter, without the preceding two adjurations (which may be why Zeeden refers to the greater exorcism as being cut), and directly followed by the reading from Mark 10.]

[185] Ramge, 110, with source texts.

people there clung to it steadfastly and in 1615 were still taking their children out of the area to be baptized by non-Reformed parsons.[186] The battle over exorcism between Lutherans and Reformed, however in part also within the Lutheran Church itself, lasted for more than a century, until in the end Rationalism and the Enlightenment disposed of this part of the old baptismal liturgy, as well as the *abrenuntiatio*.[187]

Concerning the Roman Catholic custom of the *Benedictio mulieris post partum*, or churching of women six weeks after childbirth, the church orders had varying views. This was the liturgical act of giving thanks for the birth of the child and the preservation of the mother's health. Several orders strictly rejected this act, mostly moved by the thought that it involved either useless or harmful institutions of the papacy. Thus in 1540 the visitors in the rural district of Meissen also forbade the ceremony for churching women after childbirth right along with "sprinkling, consecrating salt and water, and tolling during storms."[188] The 1569 church order of

---

[186] Götz, *Wirren*, 334. Also instructive is the description of a Calvinistic Baptism by a Lutheran; Georg Faber, personal physician of Landgrave Philipp of Hessen-Butzbach, accompanied his lord in 1632 on a trip through Detmold and there took part in the Baptism of a newborn child from the Reformed house of the counts of Lippe; he wrote about this: "At one in the afternoon a sermon was preached in the hall and the usual Gospel for the feast of Trinity was treated, then the parson stood behind the table at the window and mentioned among other things that just like water washes away all external filth, so also in Baptism the Holy Spirit cleanses us. He concluded the prayer in the same way, then the sponsors and emissaries were led to the table, upon which there was a gilded silver basin with water. During the Baptism the parson neither carried out the usual ceremonies nor asked the sponsors the questions about the Christian Creed, rather he spoke the Creed himself. After this he asked the name of the child, which had been named Simon Philipps. Then the parson baptized him while he was in the arms of his princely grace, since he did not want to take him into his Calvinistic hands." Walter Gunzert (ed.), *Skizzen- und Reisetagebuch eines Arztes im Dreißigjährigen Krieg* (Darmstadt: Darmstädter Echo, 1952), 23.
[187] Graff 1:249ff. Cf. also the extensive material in Wilken, 48ff. [Cf. Bodo Nischan, "The Exorcism Controversy and Baptism in the Late Reformation," *Sixteenth Century Journal* 18.1 (1987): 31–52.]
[188] Sehling 1:565. [Zeeden modified the confusing text here to read almost the same as at Sehling 1:625 and 2:262 as well as 1:285 and 654 (which include tolling for the souls of the faithful departed, see note 292 below);

Wolfenbüttel in contrast included in its agenda a relatively extensive section "Concerning the women who have just given birth" and described positively how this act could be interpreted evangelically.[189] Some church orders from Brandenburg and Silesia set fees for churching women six weeks after childbirth, which means that it was done there.[190] In Schleswig-Holstein the 1542 church order was totally silent about it (just like many other church orders); from parallel sources, however, it is clear that the rite of churching was maintained; among other things it consisted of the young mother going around the altar in the company of a few women and laying down an offering there.[191]

As far as the Catholic sacrament of confirmation is concerned, its stronger echoes were preserved by only one church order that I know of, namely, the 1540 church order of Electoral Brandenburg. In it Elector Joachim II appointed the time of Easter and Pentecost for confirmation and reserved it in principle for the evangelical bishop—who could, however, delegate the authority to confirm to parsons, "since," as it said, "there are many people in our lands (God be praised) and few bishops." Nonetheless the clergy entrusted with confirmation were regularly to be placed under the supervision of

---

these are all from 1540. Note 9 in Sehling 11:44f. says that consecration of salt and water occurred early every Sunday morning, therefore the formularies for this are at the front of every medieval missal. The consecrated salt was used for consecrating water and at Baptism, while consecrated water was used for an exceptionally wide variety of sprinklings. Thus "sprinkling" in our quote here could refer to the use of consecrated water for dedicating or consecrating various things, such as graves (Sehling 4:37, 1525 Prussia, and Sehling 6/1:391, 1528 Braunschweig), bells and church walls (Sehling 6/1:426, 1528 Braunschweig), herbs and candles, and more (Sehling 3:88, 1540 Mark Brandenburg, and Sehling 11:203, 1533 Brandenburg and Nürnberg). For more on tolling during storms, see note 293 below.]

[189] Sehling 6/1:163f.
[190] Gardelegen 1541 [Brandenburg], Freudenthal and Goldstein 1591 [Silesia]; Sehling 3:220 and 480.
[191] Feddersen, 486f.; Feddersen, 414: In the sixteenth century this offering tended to be rather significant on account of the number of accompanying women and meant a respectable income for the parson. [Susan C. Karant-Nunn notes that her "research indicates that the new mother did not invariably circle the altar." *The Reformation of Ritual: An Interpretation of Early Modern Germany* by (London; New York: Routledge, 1997), 23 n. 4.]

episcopal scholars, who were to "observe the parsons to make sure they handle the matter properly."[192] The purpose of the confirmation act in this church order remained close to the Catholic understanding: When the faithful and baptized have grown up, they should be examined concerning their faith; insofar as they have been found sure in their faith, the bishop should lay his hands on them, make the sign of the cross on their forehead ("to show that they should receive the cross of Christ and not be ashamed of it") and pray over them to "remain steadfast, preserved, and become even stronger" in the true faith and Christian living. A certain affinity with the Catholic rite was also noticeable in Bucer's confirmation formula (1539 church order of Hesse), which read: "Receive the Holy Spirit, the guard and shield against all evil, strength and help for all good, from the gracious hand of God. . . ." This formula passed into a large number of church orders in northern, western, and southwestern Germany and kept alive a weak remembrance of confirmation as a sacramental act.[141] Many church orders viewed confirmation purely catechetically, like the large and influential 1580 church order of Electoral Saxony. The 1552 church order for Prussian lands concisely formulated what this meant: "Instead of confirmation, diligently train the youth everywhere during Lent, particularly in the catechism, and administer the venerable sacrament of the Lord's Supper to those who are ready and able on Maundy Thursday, and then regard them as confirmed Christians."[194] Occasionally the church orders also contained polemics against the old Catholic confirmation rite.[195]

Concerning engagement, which of course was never a sacrament but was an indispensable prerequisite of marriage, it was remarkable that it was still regarded as a legally binding act, just like in the pre-Reformation period. According to the Augsburg ritual books from 1487 and 1547, the first act within the framework of a pre-Reformation church marriage consisted of a *"copulatio sponsi et*

---

[192] Sehling 3:59. [After "properly" the order continues, "and not turn it back into an abuse or frivolity, as happened before." The order also makes provision for confirmation to occur at another convenient time in the event that it cannot be done at Easter or Pentecost.]

[193] Graff 1:316 with further references. [The formula continues: "the Father and the Son and the Holy Spirit. Amen" (cf. Richter 1:304).]

[194] Sehling 2:156.

[195] References in Wilken, 52 note 292.

sponsae in domo," a legally binding blessing of the bridal couple [at home], which did not necessarily have to be by a priest. Lutheranism took over this form and embellished it festively and liturgically. Backing out of one's engagement was a crime and punished with imprisonment or exile. For all that, the people punished in this way were also required to enter into the promised marriage.[196] Secret engagements and clandestine marriages must have been a widespread custom or abuse before as well as after the Reformation. Otherwise the church orders would not have been so extensively occupied with them.[197] For the marriage ceremony itself, a church wedding was not yet regarded as absolutely essential in sixteenth century Lutheranism, whereas in the seventeenth century a public churchly confirmation of the wedding was regarded as necessary. The development here proceeded similarly to that in Catholicism since the Council of Trent. Consecration of the betrothed on the wedding day was already the rule in the Middle Ages, however, and Lutheranism took over this rule. Likewise it took over the term "*Brautmesse* (nuptial mass)," but not the Catholic rite with which it was bound. "*Brautmesse*" meant rather the church attendance of the newlyweds on the day after the wedding, at which, following a sermon on the estate of marriage, they knelt before the altar and the clergyman spoke a prayer and blessing while holding his hands over them.[198] In the direction of church law, however, none too great a difference existed between the Lutheran and the Catholic practice in matters of marriage. Not only because the ecclesiastical court was in favor of concerning itself with marriage and, as the responsible entity, of ruling in questions of doubt and

---

[196] 1585 Lauenburg and 1584 Prussia church orders; Sehling 4:133; 5:440f. [For the Augsburg ritual book Alfred Niebergall says (p. 17, note 18 in *Die Geschichte der evangelischen Trauung in Hessen*, Göttingen: Vandenhoeck & Ruprecht, 1972) that according to *Lehrbuch der Liturgik* (by Georg Rietschel, 2nd ed., rev. by Paul Graff, Vol. 2: *Die Kasualien*, Göttingen: Vandenhoeck & Ruprecht, 1952, p. 697) there are four different acts of the priest, the first of which is the "*Copulatio*," etc., but according to *Handbuch der katholischen Liturgik* (by Ludwig Eisenhofer, 2nd ed., Vol. 2: *Spezielle Liturgik*, Freiburg im Breisgau: Herder, 1941, p. 415), the first act took place in the family circle and did not require the presence of a priest. If one was present, he assisted without wearing a surplice and stole and spoke only a prayer.]
[197] Cf. the references in Wilken, 54–58.
[198] Graff 1:335.

cases of error, but also because the norms and interpretations resembled one another. The church orders knew the same hindrances to marriage posed by kinship and affinity as canon law and published precise tables in order to make known the forbidden degrees; they knew of Lent and Advent as closed times and prohibited weddings during them, and in general, aside from complicated special cases, they also regarded marriage as indissoluble.[199]

Ordination[200] likewise contains more or less remote parallels to the Catholic consecration of priests.[201] The bishop ceased to be the only one authorized to consecrate, but soon the question of legitimizing those ordaining within Lutheranism came up for discussion. The general superintendents frequently sought to claim this privilege for themselves alone and to tear it away from the superintendents; the general superintendent of Pomerania, Johann Knipstro, thought that someone should be allowed to ordain only if he himself had been ordained to the office of ordaining others. For this he called upon the biblical example of Titus, whom the Apostle Paul installed as head bishop or general superintendent of Crete, so that he in turn would install other bishops and elders, the same as superintendents, into the office there.[202] It can also be mentioned that at the ordination, aside from the ordaining minister, at least two local clergymen (and in the case of illness, substitutes from the neighboring communities) were to be present. It was also not all that different

---

[199] The examples in Sehling are so numerous that I refrain from giving individual references.

[200] The 1562 visitation instruction for the Archbishopric of Magdeburg, Sehling 2:409; in Frankfurt an der Oder in the district of the former Lebus diocese, evangelical *"Primizen"* [*Primiz* is the first Mass of a newly ordained priest] were celebrated in 1591 according to a Catholic book of rites from 1514, Heinrich Grimm, "Die liturgischen Drucke der Diözese Lebus," *Wichmann-Jahrbuch* 9/10 (1956), 51. Referring back to the 1569 church order, the 1569 order for the Wolfenbüttel monastery said that it contained guidelines for how the clergy are "ordained, consecrated, and confirmed" for the Office of the Ministry "according to the laudable ancient Christian, apostolic, and catholic church custom" Sehling 6/1:283.

[201] For more on Lutheran ordination, see Ralph F. Smith's *Luther, Ministry, and Ordination Rites in the Early Reformation Church*. New York: Peter Lang, 1996. The contrast with Catholic consecration of priests is discussed on p. 61ff. – KGW

[202] Graff 1:391.

from the old consecration of priests in that, as a legal act of the church within a liturgical act, it gave the authority to preach and administer the sacraments. Such an authority as Johann Gerhard still did not shy away from calling it a sacrament in the wide sense.[203]

Finally, it is least mistakable that Catholic traditions solidified in confession and absolution. In the early years of the Reformation Luther himself still held the view that absolution has a sacramental character; Melanchthon expressed himself unequivocally on this in the Apology,[204] and the church orders appear to have followed him more than Luther in this point. Some, such as the 1540 and 1572 church orders of Electoral Brandenburg, sought urgently to commend confession while avoiding compulsory confession.[205] Yet in many others, for example in the 1564 and 1569 Lüneburg and Wolfenbüttel church orders of Lower Saxony, an unequivocal compulsory confession prevailed: "Therefore no one shall go to the Sacrament of the Altar unless he has first gone to the priest and confessed himself as a sinner and received private absolution."[206] The sacramental character also became much clearer in these orders. The parsons were forbidden from absolving the unrepentant and admitting them to Communion, "for Christ commanded not only to loose, but also to bind." To the repentant, however, they should say with reference to Matt. 18:18, "Upon this promise of God and according to His command I declare you free of all your sins here in the stead of God in the name of the Father and of the Son and of the Holy Spirit. Amen."[207]

While private confession remained in German Lutheranism exceptionally long,[208] the anointing of the sick disappeared very early, insofar as it happened at all—and even then it was only isolated. Evidence for saying anything about this is very weak. Nikolaus

---

[203] Graff 1:390.

[204] See note 176 above.

[205] Sehling 3:61.

[206] Sehling 6/1:166.

[207] Sehling 6/1:166f., 560. The 1542 Schleswig-Holstein church order also construed the absolution as a sacramental act and cognition of the Office of the Keys.

[208] Ernst Salomon Cyprian, one of the last great orthodox churchmen in the century of the Enlightenment, believed it was instituted by God. In 1749 he published a scholarly investigation meant to prove his conviction. Graff 1:379.

Müller[209] does not regard as implausible the news that during the Interim Johann Agricola still repeatedly administered unction as a sacrament.[210] Apart from that, there is no particular need to wonder that the anointing of the sick disappeared without a sound; even within the realm of the Catholic Church back then it had largely fallen into oblivion.[211] The unction-related practice of making sick calls, however, did not entirely cease; it lived on in Lutheranism as communion of the sick. The great importance attached particularly to it becomes evident in that there is hardly a church order without a section on communing the sick. The practice of holding burning candles or handing one to the dying on this occasion, as in the Upper Palatinate, may also have been a throwback from the pre-Reformation period.[212] The act of communing the sick consisted in brief instruction in the faith with an admonition about the Sacrament, reception of the Lord's Supper, and an instructive pastoral address.[213]

For burial, most of the Catholic ceremonies fell away with the requiem mass because the doctrine of purgatory and prayer for the dead were suspect for the reformers. What remained was the simple procession from the house of the deceased into the church and to the cemetery, with a cross leading the way, and—within limits—intercessions for the deceased; these prayers were regarded by Luther and Bugenhagen as justifiable insofar as they were prayed privately, and by the Apology they were even permitted publicly.[214] The funeral sermon offered or was supposed to offer a substitute for the requiem mass, which was no longer read; in order to give the procession into the church the character of a divine service, there was also the singing of a collect and reading of a Bible passage at the altar.[215]

---

[209] Müller, 466.

[210] Cf. Gustav Kawerau, *Johann Agricola von Eisleben* (Berlin: Hertz, 1881), 277f.

[211] It was unknown in 1625 in an ecclesiastically-sound Benedictine monastery in the chapter domain of Osnabrück, Herzebrock. Franz Flaskamp, *Die Kirchenvisitation des Albert Lucenius im Archidiakonat Wiedenbrück (1625): zur Reformationsgeschichte des Hochstifts Osnabrück* (Wiedenbrück, Hanhardt, 1952), 53f.

[212] Götz, *Wirren*, 355.

[213] Feddersen, 484f. [Also see "exhortation" in the index.]

[214] Graff 1:255ff., 360; *BSLK*, 375f. [Art. XXIV, 94–96.]

[215] Feddersen, 488f. [For a more detailed account of Lutheran rituals surrounding death, the reader is referred to Craig Koslofsky's *The

Finally, we also mention that, just as in the Catholic period, consecration acts were carried out for churches, parts of churches, and worship objects, such as altars, bells, and baptismal fonts, and that several older traditions continued to operate here. The same was true, at least in part, for church dedication festivals and patron saint days. The ritual book used for such sometimes agreed with the Catholic one; for example, with some texts (Numbers 10:1–3: trumpets shall call the people together; some psalms: Ps. 24, 118, 122 Evangelical/Hebrew enumeration).[216]

ADDENDUM: SPECIAL CONDITIONS IN CATHEDRALS AND COLLEGIATE CHURCHES

Additionally it can still be pointed out that, as a modest number of Catholic traditions were generally to be encountered among the worship acts last touched upon, so also a very rich treasure of traditions was preserved in isolated areas of evangelical or half-evangelical ecclesial life; namely in the realm of some north German, often immediate[217] collegiate churches and cathedrals, whose chapters each made special rules for themselves. Here, probably due primarily to external reasons, Catholic institutions generally remained the longest: chanted prayer[218] and processions; in individual cases even celibacy, as in the Loccum monastery near Hannover, the Michael monastery in Lüneburg, and the cathedral chapter in Lübeck.[219] Individual cathedral chapters even knew of conferring evangelical lower and higher consecrations; thus Osnabrück and Havelberg.[220] The Duchy of Braunschweig-Wolfenbüttel's princely reformer, Duke Julius, had his son and successor, Heinrich Julius, receive the tonsure and consecration after he had him elected as the bishop of Halberstadt

---

Reformation of the Dead: Death and Ritual in Early Modern Germany, 1450–1700 (Basingstoke: Macmillan, 2000).]

[216] Graff 1:400–414 with much material.

[217] Directly subject to the emperor. – KGW

[218] *Chorgebet*, i.e. the daily choir offices, for which cathedral and collegiate chapter clergy would gather in the choir (chancel) to sing the canonical hour services. – KGW

[219] Sehling 6/1:628; 6/2:1006, Nottarp, 10, cf. Heckel, 42f., Hans Erich Feine, "Das protestantische Fürstbistum Lübeck," *Zeitschrift der Savigny-Stiftung für Rechtsgeschichte: kanonistische Abteilung* 11 (1921), 439ff.

[220] Nottarp, 10, Heckel, 115f.

at the age of two.[221] There were also tonsured evangelical canons in individual Westphalian collegiate chapters.[222] An evangelical bishop of Minden even swore to the *Professio fidei Tridentinae* (Profession of Faith of the Council of Trent), although he probably did so more with the intent of receiving papal confirmation in order to have less trouble gaining possession of the bishopric.[223] In the same Minden, evangelical canons took part in processions; certainly this was also done, as claimed, in order not to miss out on the money given for attendance. It is surely not permissible, however, to trace the retention of Catholic customs exclusively to such ostensible motives. Also at work in this was something of the natural inertia of deeply rooted institutions. Above all, a strong cause for such conservative behavior is to be sought in the simple fact that those imperial bishoprics and chapters between the Elbe and Rhine which had become evangelical consisted almost entirely of chapters having mixed confessions, whose Catholic and Lutheran members must have been greatly concerned with finding and practicing some sort of *modus vivendi*[224] of the common church service (*Kirchendienst*), considering that they sat so close to one another in terms of background and station in life.

---

[221] Sehling 2:464. [Sehling says he was postulated at age two and the chapter governed the bishopric until he took over at age fourteen, having received the tonsure just a week and a half before. Although the tonsure caused quite a stir in Protestant circles, Jakob Andreae declared it an adiaphoron and Duke Julius declared that his son's confessional allegiance was to the Augsburg Confession.] Annelies Ritter, "Über die Lehrstreitigkeiten in Wolfenbüttel" etc. *Jahrbuch der Gesellschaft für niedersächsiche Kirchengeschichte* 50 (1952), 87 with references.

[222] Heckel, 117.

[223] Karl Müller, *Kirchengeschichte* II/2 (Tübingen: Mohr, 1919), 283, speaks in general of false pretenses; the bishop in question is Hermann von Schauenburg, cf. *Lexikon für Theologie und Kirche* 7:195. [The pope would not confirm him as bishop unless he swore to the *Professio*; although Hermann did so, he continued to govern as a Protestant ruler (Heinrich Kampschulte, *Geschichte der Einführung des Protestantismus im Bereiche der jetzigen Provinz Westfalen. Pragmatisch dargestellt*. Paderborn: Schöningh 1866, p. 260).]

[224] "Method of living," i.e. a compromise between adversaries that allows them to get along temporarily. – KGW

IV. THE CHURCH YEAR

The celebration of the divine service was very closely associated with the course of the church year, the particular times of which each found expression in the movable or *de tempore* parts of the liturgy [the propers, which changed based on the Sunday or festival day of the church year]. Seen on the whole, the old Catholic church year unmistakably shone through the Lutheran agendas. The high feasts of the Lord, Advent and Lent as the weeks of spiritual preparation for Christmas and Easter, plus the breaks of the Ember Days[225] determined its rhythm also within the realm of Lutheranism. These were joined by a crown of other feasts and festivals, not as lavish as in the Catholic Church, yet also not poor.

Beginning with the feasts: Their number and duration varied considerably with countryside and territory, yet certain supra-local commonalities can be recognized. The duration of the high feasts was three days (in the west often only one day, for example in Landau); they were usually three in number: Christmas, Easter, and Pentecost. It also happened, though, that the feast of the archangel Michael (September 29) was celebrated as a fourth high feast; this was the case, for example, in Osnabrück, Waldeck, and Electoral Brandenburg.[226] The rest were divided into whole-day and half-day festivals; concerning which days were to be celebrated as whole or half, however, there was quite a vast disparity among the church orders. Almost without exception, the following were regarded as church festivals: the Circumcision of Christ (New Year); Epiphany (Three Kings' Day); Christ's Ascension; the three Marian feasts with a foundation in the Gospel—the Purification (Candlemas), the Annunciation, and the Visitation; John the Baptist's days (birth and beheading); the archangel Michael (and all angels); the Holy Innocents, St. Stephen, and all apostles, including Paul's conversion. In addition to this there was usually the feast of Mary Magdalene, because it concerns an event contained in the Gospel. This was, so to

---

[225] There were four annual Ember Day festivals, each three days (Wednesday, Friday, and Saturday) of preparation before the four high feasts mentioned in the next paragraph. These were times not only of fasting, prayer, and repentance, but also for ordination and giving tithes and alms to the clergy and poor. In the Lutheran Church they were used particularly for catechesis. – KGW

[226] Graff 1:113f., Müller, 535.

speak, the minimum inventory. Oddly enough, amid the rounds of apostles' feasts, the feast of Peter and Paul falls under the table in some church orders; perhaps to declare opposition to the papacy. For even if it was a trifle for a well-educated theologian to interpret the Gospel in Matthew 16 without a hint of papism, the account of the giving of the keys of the kingdom of heaven could perhaps awaken all kinds of memories among the simple people, which would be better avoided.

Beyond this standard amount, some local variations included St. Laurence, the Finding of the Cross, All Saints, and St. Martin; the Assumption of Mary was celebrated relatively often[227] and the Nativity of Mary more rarely. In certain areas Corpus Christi was also celebrated. St. Martin (November 11) not only had a firm position as a date in the agricultural year (end of harvest), but was also celebrated as a day for commemorating the Reformation and occasionally[228] also in remembrance of Martin Luther.[229] The celebration of All Saints' Day, sometimes still connected with All Souls' Day, November 1–2, was relatively widespread and apparently remained into the eighteenth century as a feast of joyful thanks for the faithful

---

[227] This may sound like more than it is. In the volumes of Sehling that were available to Zeeden, I find that retention of the Assumption of Mary is explicitly mentioned only in the 1542 Anhalt order (Sehling 2:542), the 1540/45 Mecklenburg order (Sehling 5:152), the 1565 city statutes of Görlitz (Sehling 3:376; the city is in Upper Lusatia), and the Mark Brandenburg order from 1540, 1558, and 1572 (Sehling 3:87, 91, 102; several visitation records for Mark Brandenburg also mention this). Although the 1540/45 Mecklenburg order retains the Assumption, it specifies the readings (1 Timothy 4 and Luke 10) and clarifies that they want to have nothing to do with the impious dealings of the papists. In 1523 Luther wrote that the Assumption and Nativity of Mary could still remain for a while, although the liturgical texts associated with them were impure (Concerning the Order of Public Worship, *LW* 53:14, *WA* 12:37 lines 21–23, Sehling 1:3). The Assumption is ruled out by numerous orders, such as the 1544 synodical orders for Calenburg-Göttingen (Sehling 6/2:868), the 1569 agenda for Pomerania (Sehling 4:470), and the orders in note 231 below). As Zeeden points out below, several places celebrated the day for the Assumption of Mary as the feast of the Visitation of Mary (see note 234 below). – KGW
[228] 1569 Pomeranian agenda, Sehling 4:470.
[229] References for all of the feast days passim in Sehling; cf. also the material-rich compilation in Graff 1:112–128; a compilation specifically for Amberg is in Ramge, 121f. with references.

departed.[230] Of the three Marian feasts that were not derived from Holy Scripture, the Assumption of Mary took very deep root in the consciousness of the people as an Ember Day festival.[231] The 1530 Minden church order stipulated that, although it was not grounded in the Bible, the day of the Assumption (August 15) was still to be retained for a time in view of uneducated peasants, custom, and the Ember Day dues, which were to be paid on this date.[232] For practical reasons numerous church orders transferred the feast of the Visitation (July 2), on account of its temporal proximity to Peter and Paul (July 29) and on account of the accruing harvest work,[233] to August 15, which had been naturalized as an Ember Day and festival.[234] It practically goes without saying that, with its highly conservative character, the 1540 church order of Electoral Brandenburg retained the festival. Celebration of the Nativity of Mary was more rare.[235] For celebration of the feast of the Immaculate Conception (December 8),

---

[230] Cf. the list of references in Graff 1:126.

[231] Several orders say that St. Michael is to be celebrated as an Ember Day festival instead of the Assumption of Mary, such as the 1542 Calenburg-Göttingen order (Sehling 6/2:811), the 1552 Mecklenburg order (Sehling 5:201, also a visitation document of the same year), the 1569 Braunschweig-Wolfenbüttel order (Sehling 6/1:152), and the 1581 Hoya order (Sehling 6/2:1186). The 1540/45 Mecklenburg (Sehling 5:152) and 1569 Braunschweig-Wolfenbüttel (Sehling 6/1:152) orders also speak out against a practice associated with celebration of the Assumption of Mary: the blessing of herbs, which were used for various superstitious purposes, such as warding off bad weather or healing (see also Sehling 6/1:63, 6/2:799, and *DWB* "Krautweihe"). – KGW

[232] A copy of the church order is in the *Jahrbuch des Vereins für westfälische Kirchengeschichte* 43 (1950), 48ff. [=Martin Krieg, *Die Einführung der Reformation in Minden, nebst Abdruck der Mindischen Kirchenordnung des Nicolaus Krage von 1530.* Bethel bei Bielefeld: Verlagshandlung der Amstalt Bethel, 1950.]

[233] July 2 prior to the Gregorian calendar reform = July 12.

[234] Numerous references in Graff 1:126. [See, e.g., the 1533 Nürnberg church order and Veit Dietrich's little agenda of 1545 (Sehling 11:538).]

[235] For example Brandenburg 1540 and Görlitz 1565, Sehling 3:87 and 376; cf. also Robert Lansemann, *Die Heiligentage, besonders die Marien-, Apostel- und Engeltage in der Reformationszeit: betrachtet im Zusammenhang der reformatorischen Anschauungen von den Zeremonien, von den Festen, von den Heiligen und von den Engeln* (Göttingen: Vandenhoeck & Ruprecht, 1939), 131.

however, only one example is known to me: Görlitz prescribed the celebration of this day in its municipal bylaws from 1565.[236] Furthermore, people did not usually let the celebration of particular local and city patron saints be taken from them: Bugenhagen, the creator of many north-German church orders, consciously tied in with these traditions, but simultaneously transformed them by elevating the patron saint festivals to thanksgiving feasts of a more general character. This was the case, for example, in Lübeck, Hamburg, and Braunschweig.[237] Incidentally in some places and lands Corpus Christi was also celebrated. In Unna in the County of Mark this feast continued until 1659; according to all indications, it was not removed in the Berlin cathedral chapter and perhaps generally in the Electoral Mark of Brandenburg until into the seventeenth century, since it had not been removed with the dozens of feasts during the great liturgical purging of 1598.[238] Likewise Görlitz celebrated this day.[239] In south-German imperial cities having parity[240] (Augsburg, Ravensburg) the

---

[236] Sehling 3:376; on the evangelical Marian feasts in general, cf. Lansemann (previous note), passim; and Reintraud Schimmelpfennig, *Geschichte der Marienverehrung im deutschen Protestantismus* (Paderborn: Schöningh, 1952), 34ff., 71f.

[237] Sehling 5:358 [Lübeck 1531], 515 [Hamburg 1529], 6/1:398f. [Braunschweig 1528].

[238] "[The day] of Corpus Christi can be retained with a sermon," Müller, 535f.; both church orders, the one from 1540 as well as the one from 1572, mentioned the day of Corpus Christi, or rather Coena Domini (the Lord's Supper), among the feast days to be observed: Sehling 3:87, 102.

[239] The 1565 city statutes of Görlitz (Sehling 3:376). In the volumes of Sehling that were available to Zeeden, I also find the retention of Corpus Christi mentioned in the 1542 Anhalt order (Sehling 2:542) and the 1539 city of Northeim order (Sehling 6/2:935; the city is in Lower Saxony). The latter says Corpus Christi had to be retained for a particular political reason, but the procession and all other un-Christian ceremonies are abrogated: only God's Word and the Lord's Supper are permitted to remain. Other orders say that Corpus Christi is not to be celebrated at all, such as the 1544 synodical orders for Calenburg-Göttingen (Sehling 6/2:868), the 1569 Braunschweig-Wolfenbüttel order (Sehling 6/1:152), and the 1569 agenda for Pomerania (Sehling 4:470). Sehling (3:372) says that the Corpus Christi procession in the city of Sorau (Lower Lusatia, now Żary, Poland) was abolished in 1538. – KGW

[240] "In canon law, a status of civil equality for various ecclesiastical societies. So long as the pre-Reformation heresy law in Germany was in

evangelical populace had to take part in the Catholic festivals and probably held prayer hours. In Fraustadt at the Silesian-Polish border they did so voluntarily; moreover, they did it with the beautiful, irenic reasoning that the day of Corpus Christi should be retained "for the sake of neighbors, to avoid giving offense." At the same time, they found a way to celebrate the day evangelically: Fraustadt's 1564 church order continues, "For if we do not carry around the Sacrament, since that is contrary to the Lord's institution, one can still preach and teach in the church about the Sacrament to the great benefit of the common folk."[241]

Alongside of these saints' and Lord's feasts, however, various churchly festivals, bound with the natural seasons and interspersed with popular, often superstitious acts and notions, were also preserved. Rogation days for the fruits of the field, celebrated in the Catholic Church during Rogation Week, more precisely on the three Rogation days before Christ's Ascension, lived on almost everywhere in Lutheranism as "Prayer Week" or "Cross Week." These evangelical prayer days were not all on the same dates, but fell

---

force, there was no such thing as parity; but in 1555, after the Peace of Augsburg, the German empire declared the heresy law to be no longer applicable. A distinction remains, however, to be drawn between parity guaranteed by the German empire and the measures adopted by its constituent state governments; the empire never prescribed that the two confessional bodies should be placed on a footing of equality by the respective states. Parity signifies solely an equality of treatment for Roman Catholic and Protestant estates of the realm in matters of the empire's jurisdiction." *The New Schaff-Herzog Encyclopedia of Religious Knowledge*, vol. 8, p. 356 (ed. by Samuel M. Jackson, Grand Rapids: Baker Book House, 1953). For more on imperial cities and their role in the Reformation, see *The Negotiated Reformation: Imperial Cities and the Politics of Urban Reform, 1525–1550* by Christopher W. Close (Cambridge; New York: Cambridge University Press, 2009). – KGW

[241] Graff 1:125; Sehling 3:376 [Görlitz 1565]; 4:293f. (Fraustadt), which notes that a later addition to the church book at this point records that the feast fell out of use many years ago and, "because it is market day [*marktag*] and the doctrine of the Sacrament is treated with greater benefit on Palm Sunday, it was not reestablished." For substantiation of Lutheran veneration of saints: soteriologically as God's coworkers; exemplarily as bearers of the Holy Spirit and as models of Christian faith and striving for virtue, the reader is referred to Ramge, 121 (where there are further references) and Lansemann, *Die Heiligentage* etc. [note 235 above], passim.

without exception in the period between Easter and Pentecost and were mostly concentrated around either May 1 or the Ascension. The prayer intention was everywhere focused on successful crops, temporal preservation, protection in every need, "and other necessary things" (Pappenheim church order). The liturgy of these prayer days included the Litany.[242] St. John's Fire also fit into the rhythm of the church year; it was used to drive livestock on St. John [the Baptist's] Day in Lower Germany, in order to protect them from diseases. The church orders did not like to see this and condemned it as heathen and papistic.[243] The hail festivals or hail fire were handled differently. Living on in them was the pre-Christian cultic custom of lighting a fire before the beginning of summer, which was supposed to ban from the fields future danger by hail or thunderstorms. While the Pomeranian agenda of 1569 called such hail festivals idolatry and threatened those who organized them with exclusion from the sacraments,[244] they were celebrated without objection in various places in northwestern Germany.[245]

Incidentally, how close Lutheranism remained to the Catholic Church in taking over festivals becomes perfectly clear when drawing in Calvinism for comparison: The Reformed not only rejected the feasts of the church year, but also ignored them ostentatiously and provocatively, for example, when they diligently preached about the Holy Spirit at Christmas, or about the wedding in Cana during Passiontide.[246] They also abrogated the pericopes, whereas the Lutherans took over the Catholic order of pericopes with minor alterations. A main representative of Lutheran orthodoxy in the eighteenth century, Valentin Ernst Löscher (1673 to 1749), held vigils and spiritual meditations before the church festivals and refrained from eating meat on ancient church fasting days.[247]

---

[242] Graff 1:138ff., cf. also the 1581 Braunschweig-Grubenhagen church order in Sehling 6/2:1079ff.

[243] For example the 1569 Pomeranian agenda, Sehling 4:470; more in Wilken, 87.

[244] Sehling 4:470.

[245] In Dortmund, Hohenlimburg, Essen, and the Soest Tract (*Börde*) [all in the County of Mark], Graff 1:138; in Essen, three half-day hail festivals were celebrated on the three Fridays following Pentecost, Graff 1:138.

[246] Graff 1:129 and note 5 there.

[247] Graff 1:129f.

What has been said about saints' days and feasts in particular applied to the church year as a whole: Its essential components passed into Lutheranism. It underwent some changes in content and the way it was celebrated; however, it remained intact in its structure and order, with its rhythms and tides. Advent, Lent, Passiontide, and even the Ember Days retained their character as times of special reflection and immersion in the salvation event. Of course their peculiar character was taken into account in a way other than before the Reformation: Not the liturgy, but the sermon and catechesis should promote the special religious stimulation and immersion. In Advent in Amberg, for example, alongside the respective Gospel texts the promises of the Old Testament were to be diligently included in the readings.[248] Almost every Lutheran church order contained comparable directions. From the evangelical Passion-piety gradually grew the particularly dignified celebration of Good Friday; corresponding more with Catholic tradition, however, Good Friday in the sixteenth century still did not by any means occupy a special position.

Similar to the retention of St. Martin's Day, remembrance of the Ember Days stayed alive more due to external reasons. These days had so firmly naturalized themselves and also played such a significant role as breaks in the course of the agricultural financial year that, even if someone had wanted to abrogate them, that could not have been done very easily. The traditional quarterly or Ember Day fee continued to be paid, and this was monitored by the authorities.

Lent (*Fastenzeit*, Fastingtide) was preserved in the vocabulary of the church orders, as far as I can tell, without exception. It served especially as a time for instruction in the catechism. The 1564 church order from Zittau expressed itself totally in keeping with the tenor of the Lutheran church orders when it "laudably" prescribed "that the catechism be preached on every day of the week during Lent at *Salve* times[249]; these sermons on the catechism should also be held as they

---

[248] Ramge, 123.

[249] According to Sehling 6/1:599 note 34, the *Salve Regina* antiphon is supposed to have been composed by Hermann Contractus (d. 1054) and used since the beginning of the thirteenth century chiefly in connection with the canonical hours, sometimes also after the Mass was sung. For the Latin text, cf. *Liber Usualis* p. 276 or 279. Gradually it became a rather popular practice

were initiated, always, firmly, and without exception."[250] Occasionally "Fastingtide" remained in its actual sense, thus not just

---

to hold *Salve Regina* devotions separate from the hours and the Mass. Foundations were frequently made to this end. Attendance was promoted by granting of indulgences. Sehling refers to Stephan Beissel, *Geschichte der Verehrung Marias im 16. und 17. Jahrhundert: Ein Beitrag zur Religionswissenschaft und Kunstgeschichte* (Freiburg im Breisgau: Herder, 1910) pp. 494–505 and Ludwig Eisenhofer, *Handbuch der katholischen Liturgik*, Vol. 2: *Spezielle Liturgik* (Freiburg im Breisgau: Herder, 1933), p. 553f. For an example of such a *Salve Regina* foundation, see p. 103f. in *Wittelsbach Court in Munich: History and Authority in the Visual Arts (1460–1508)* (Andreas M. Dahlem, Ph.D. diss., Univ. of Glasgow, 2009). Sehling 6/1:517 note 33a refers to foundations of other Marian devotions.

Martin Luther drew attention to the *Salve Regina* in a sermon on the Nativity of Mary on Sept. 8, 1522: "Likewise concerning the holy Virgin Mary in the *Salve*. What are those for words attributed to her? 'Hail, queen of mercy, our life, our sweetness, and our hope.' Is that not too much? Who will answer for her supposedly being our life, our mercy, and our sweetness, when she herself is content with being a lowly vessel? This prayer is sung throughout the whole world and is accompanied by the tolling of big bells. This is also how it is with the *Regina celi*; calling her a queen of heaven is no better. Is it not doing Christ a dishonor to attribute to a creature that which is due to God alone?" (*WA* 10/3:321 lines 7–10 and 322 lines 1–5). Regarding the bell tolling associated with the *Salve Regina*, see note 288 below. For the Latin text of *Regina caeli*, cf. *Liber Usualis* p. 275 or 278. For more on the role of Mary in the church at this time, see *The Cult of the Virgin Mary in Early Modern Germany: Protestant and Catholic Piety, 1500–1648* by Bridget Heal (Cambridge; New York: Cambridge University Press, 2007).

Although one finds statements like "The *salve regina* shall not be sung, for it serves to minimize God" (Sehling 4:29, 1525 *Themata episcopi Risenburgensis*; Riesenburg, Duchy of Prussia is now Prabuty, Poland) and "Singing of the *salve* shall be entirely abolished" (Sehling 1:672, 1555 church order for Senftenberg, Electoral Saxony), not all were strictly opposed to it. The 1524 Coburg order concerning services says the *Salve* is to be retained, "but with renewal of the words in accordance with Holy Scripture" (Sehling 1:543). In the same year, Sebald Heyden, rector of the *Spitalschule* in Nürnberg, rewrote the *Salve Regina* to give it an evangelical sense and proceeded to use it in the Saturday evening *Salve* services, for which there was a foundation. This sparked a serious literary battle (Sehling 11:18, with references). – KGW

[250] Sehling 3:379. [Similarly, the 1577 Gottleuba church order states that, "Every day in Lent, starting with the first Sunday, when the idolatrous *salve*

as a period of the church year, but rather as abstinence from food and the eating of meat; in individual cases even for quite a long time, as the example of Valentin Ernst Löscher[251] showed. Although it was regarded as good from a religious angle, the responsible authorities also gladly motivated it—if they motivated it at all—with educational and economic considerations. The imperial city of Nordhausen issued a fasting law prohibiting consumption of meat within a policy order (*Polizeiordnung*) in 1549.[252] Elector Moritz of Saxony did not directly command fasting, but nonetheless forbade, also in 1549, slaughtering and selling meat during Quadragesima (Lent).[253] Both decrees apparently were connected with the Interim. They motivated the meat prohibition by raising prices in the land. Moreover, the Nordhausen policy order regarded it as good expressly to declare that it was no sin and not forbidden by God to eat meat at the specified times; if they forbade it anyhow, this was for disciplinary reasons, or to say it in the actual words of the decree: "We . . . have sought and desired nothing more in this than obedience and good order, policy, and moderation." By contrast, the 1542 church order for the Barony of Seidenberg in Lusatia[254] decreed, independently of the Interim, that fasting should take place every Wednesday and Friday.[255] A similar ruling appears to have occurred in 1569 in Ostrorog in the former Province of Posen.[256] The Electoral Brandenburg church order of 1540, on the other hand, was particularly detailed and comprehensive. Here it said that fasting is good for many reasons: first, because the youth and simple folk have to become accustomed to depriving themselves of nourishment once in a while; second, since the people are inherently inclined to gluttony, it behooves a good authority to put a curb in place to wean

---

regina was sung in the papacy, catechesis will be held with the children every day until Palm Sunday" (Sehling 1:569).]

[251] See the sentence at note 247 above.

[252] Sehling 2:396. [The order does not expressly prohibit, but says instead: "we want everyone also to refrain from eating meat two times a week during Lent, Fridays and Saturdays, except for old sick people, hard laborers, young children, women who just gave birth, or people permitted by doctor's order, yet no one should seek in this any wantonness or abuse." Nordhausen is in Thuringia.]

[253] Sehling 1:102.

[254] Seidenberg was in Upper Lusatia; now it is Zawidów, Poland. – KGW

[255] Sehling 3:366.

[256] Sehling 4:300 [now it is Ostroróg, Poland].

the folk from drinking and gorging; third, however, one should consider that Mark Brandenburg is a land rich in fish, and therefore it is good and useful, precisely in spring, when meat is "unseasonable," to avail oneself of this abundance. Thus in Brandenburg the Quadragesima as well as all festivals and Saturdays were elevated to days of fasting and abstinence from meat.[257] With these rulings the 1540 church order hardly differed in practice from the fasting regulations in Catholic lands, with which, incidentally, they also agreed in decrees with exceptions for the sick and weak (who were granted meat when they presented certificates).[258] If fasting was urged by virtue of political decree here, as in Saxony, Nordhausen, Seidenberg, etc., that of course still did not say anything about the extent to which these guidelines were actually observed, but rather only made evident the tendency of the government. Then again, within the population itself, which often joyfully disregarded the churchly food prohibitions in the initial years of the Reformation, and of whose gluttony the elector of Brandenburg was not the only one to complain, some of the stricter old customs remained in effect even longer. In 1579–83 and 1615 there were repeatedly individuals in the Upper Palatinate who, according to the visitors' reports, observed the fasting days and did not eat any meat on Fridays or even in the whole of Lent.[259]

With these pieces of information we end our overview of the church year and now turn our attention to the broader realm of ceremonies and worship acts and customs in the more remote sense.

---

[257] *Fast- und Abstinenztage* generally meant eating only once on a fasting day and abstaining from meat. – KGW

[258] Sehling 3:87f. The special ruling for the sick and weak is also in the Nordhausen policy order, Sehling 2:396. The 1570 Kurland church order also contained secular-disciplinary and religious viewpoints, Sehling 5:92: a) It recommended fasting multiple times a week on the basis of Matt. 6:17 as "salutary, beneficial, necessary, and very good," and praying "zealously, fervently, and devoutly," "so that the flesh does not become too strong for the spirit"; b) it thought that, given the distresses of the present, it would indeed be fitting for Christian authorities if, following the example "of many Christian and saintly regents," they "would institute some special fasting days for the impious people" and would watch over their observance with an iron rod, so that "this kind of devil . . . might be driven out by fasting and prayer [and so that] God's burning anger might be stayed."

[259] Götz, *Wirren*, 88, 299.

V. FURTHER DEVOTIONAL CUSTOMS: SPIRITUAL PLAYS, PROCESSIONS, PILGRIMAGES, BELL TOLLS DURING STORMS

The survival of older churchly customs was more richly documented in the visitation reports and records than in the church orders. Nevertheless, it is possible to conclude with some degree of certainty from the church orders which older churchly traditions remained in practice, at least in such cases where they contrasted with a particular situation or particular events that they described, approved, or deplored. For example in Baruth, a city that was located near the Spreewald and at that time belonged to the electoral district (*Kurkreis*) of Saxony, as is evident from an order issued in 1529, when a parson complained "that the villages have many Wendish farmers, who are stubborn, coarse people and, even though the Lord's Gospel has been preached for about four years in Baruth, they still offer opposition and refuse to receive the Sacrament under both kinds,"[260] the sincerity of this communication warrants even less doubt than the guidelines that the local clergyman received in reply, which were entirely tailored to the existence and future correction of this situation.[261] Cautious conclusions can also be drawn from frequently repeating prohibitions and penal regulations, even if the border between the concrete and the stereotypical is not always clearly recognizable here. However, when a church order like the one for the Principality of Teschen in the former Austria-Silesia in the year 1584, that is, after more than four decades of Protestantism in this territory, complains that at the Mass, especially in villages, "many idolatrous ceremonies were kept and are still being kept," and cited further particulars of this: "adoration of the Sacrament, enclosing the Sacrament in a ciborium" . . . "elevation and ostension" . . . "processions with banners and more of such idolatry, especially the idolatrous abuse during Passion Week with the making of graves and singing before them," then it can surely be concluded from such a

---

[260] Sehling 1:524. [*evangelium dominicale* is read here as "the Lord's Gospel" instead of "the Sunday Gospel."]

[261] He was enjoined never to administer the Sacrament to anyone from that time forth unless it was under both kinds. Furthermore, he was to preach and teach them more clearly and more often at fitting times about the proper use of the Sacrament and how Christ instituted it. Sehling 1:524. – KGW

portrayal of the situation that the old Catholic rites still blossomed here considerably.[262] A parallel example is offered by the critique of Lutheran theologians at the service of the Berlin cathedral chapter, who pleaded for someone to put an end to the spiritual spectacles, especially during Passion Week, with the many processions and the pomp put on display in them, the bishop's hat and staff carried around in them, with the washing of feet on Maundy Thursday, and with the many festivals. This critique designates such customs as causing scandal and demands their removal for the sake of posterity, in order that—in Luther's words[263]—"such a stench from the pope might not cause new damage to the soul."[264] Such remarks inadvertently document that the ordinances of Joachim II pertaining to this in the 1540 church order did not just stay on paper, but were actually observed and remained until the end of the century.[265] These plays, significantly called re-presentations, were supposed to represent the salvation event during Passion Week and on high feast days in simple, graphic acts; this included, for instance, bringing a wooden donkey into the church on Palm Sunday, or pouring water down from the roof of the church on the feast of Pentecost, perhaps even throwing down fire or releasing doves. Of course the people also had all kinds of fun, mischief, and other amusements with this, which could be quite lacking spiritually.[266] On the other hand, the graphic nature offered the people of an illiterate era a foundation and

---

[262] Sehling 3:461.

[263] Exposition of the prophet Micah 5, *Opera.* Tom VIII (Wittenberg: Schwenck, 1568), fol. 501b. [This quote does not appear in either of the two versions of the exposition of Micah in *WA* 13, as it is a German translation of Veit Dietrich's Latin compilation of Luther's lectures. While it appears to be an addition of Dietrich, he gave the Micah manuscript to Luther prior to publication (*WA* 13:XXX). The title of *Opera* Tom VIII begins with *Der Achte Teil der Buecher des Ehrwirdigen Herrn D. Martini Lutheri* and has been assigned BVB number VD0080459, but has not been digitalized to date (http://www.gateway-bayern.de). Instead one may refer to Vol. 6, col. 2929 of *D. Martin Luthers Sämtliche Schriften*, ed. by Johann Georg Walch (Halle: Gebauer, 1741).]

[264] Müller, 531ff.; the quote is on p. 536.

[265] Cf. Sehling 3:88.

[266] In the pre-Reformation period Bishop Wedego of Havelberg prohibited liturgical plays already in 1471, because of the buffoonery that occurred with them, Müller, 512f.

concentration aids for devotion, which applied above all to the washing of feet, or to the Maundy Thursday or Good Friday acts before the groups communing and the portrayals of the holy tomb in the churches. This view was expressly represented, for example, by the 1540 Brandenburg church order, which warned against abuses and exuberances, yet at the same time allowed the "spectacle" to continue on Ascension, Pentecost, and other days, because "such spectacles are good reminders for the youth and the ignorant."[267]

Processions in particular were among the popular religious customs, and the people must have also felt a relatively strong need for making pilgrimages, especially since personal needs and desires of a most rudimentary nature were involved here. The processions or "rounds" also remained on a modest scale almost without exception in Lutheran churches: for church dedication acts, for example, or also during the Cross or Prayer Week,[268] likewise also for burial acts, since the matter itself demanded it, so to speak.[269] Participation in Catholic processions was no rarity in confessionally-mixed cathedral and collegiate chapters, even among members of evangelical chapters.[270] Over and above that, however, processions also occurred here and there in Lutheran regions. The most impressive example of this is offered again by Mark Brandenburg, and among its cities preeminently Berlin. Nikolaus Müller furnished proof that over a hundred processions took place annually in Berlin until about 1600, year after year on the forenoon of every Sunday and festival; additionally in the afternoon on special feasts; besides this also on certain days like Mark's Day, during Rogation Week before Ascension, and on Corpus Christi. The processions that were not limited to the cathedral, but required broader participation on solemn occasions—not only of all clergy from Berlin and Kölln, but also at the elector's behest all schoolboys, all girls older than ten, and the village clergy within an eighteen-mile radius of Berlin—exhibited noisy pomp and a rich display of splendor: Every clergyman was vested and had a chalice and paten; the cathedral provost was followed by the Prussian eagle and a banner with the Prussian coat of arms (the elector's co-investiture with Prussia had just occurred);

---

[267] Sehling 3:88.
[268] Cf. the examples in Graff 1:141, 402ff.
[269] Examples in Graff 1:355ff.
[270] Nottarp, 16, Heckel, 111.

after this came the elector high upon a horse and wearing a garment of brocade lined with sable.[271]

If the processions corresponded more to a festive desire and perhaps a natural pleasure in spectating, the making of pilgrimages went back to rudimentary religious impulses. According to the view of the Reformation, of course, these impulses were misguided, and therefore pilgrimages were not regarded as adiaphora, but were strictly opposed. People made pilgrimages to holy sites, usually to those at which something miraculous had occurred, either to make personal requests, or to give thanks in fulfillment of a vow, also in order to do penance or make satisfaction. This practice—which had been going on for centuries and been handed down from generation to generation, and about whose efficacy supposedly the most positive convictions circulated—enjoyed such popularity and prevalence in the Middle Ages that it really would have been a wonder had it met its end in one fell swoop. The opposite was also supposedly the case in an age so deeply sunk in superstition[272] and in which folly and faith in miracles often strangely mixed. Thus the making of pilgrimages, although altogether forbidden, was apparently not brought down so quickly. (If the people insisted on making a pilgrimage, surely they often did so in all secrecy.) There were complaints about the people's propensity for worshiping the Sacrament, making pilgrimages, and adoring devotional images in Upper and Middle Baden,[273] in the

---

[271] Müller, 509ff. [Note that Zeeden's description here blends Müller's account of the procession for the first Reformation festival in Berlin (1563) and again after the elector's co-investiture (1569), thus it is not the picture of a typical procession. Zeeden and Müller say four *Meilen*, but it is unclear which German *Meile*. Converting four *Meilen* of 7500 meters into our miles of 5280 feet results in 18.6 miles.]

[272] See below, Chapter 3, Section 2, Part b, "Popular customs, superstition, witchcraft" (after note 390).

[273] Upper and Middle Baden are not well-defined terms. For our purposes, Upper Baden can be taken as the two small southern portions on the map, now referred to as Markgräflerland (including cities such as Emmendingen, Sulzburg, Weil am Rhein, and Lörrach), while Middle Baden can be taken as the northmost portion on the map (including cities such as Karlsruhe, Durlach, Pforzheim, and Baden-Baden); in the sixteenth century, Baden-Baden was referred to as the Upper Margraviate and Baden-Durlach as the Lower Margraviate. – KGW

Electoral Palatinate,[274] and in the rural district of Ulm.[275] The princes of Mecklenburg prohibited it in 1552; the Duke of Lauenburg, Franz II, still thought it necessary in 1585 to make pilgrimages and the vows associated with them punishable.[276] Similar prohibitions were thought necessary in Ernestine Thuringia in the mid-sixteenth century, and still thought appropriate even in the mid-seventeenth century in the County of Hanau-Lichtenberg.[277] The Lutheran and Calvinistic visitation acts from the later sixteenth and early seventeenth century worked on by Johann Baptist Götz for the Upper Palatinate enable us to gain a clearer insight into this level of popular piety in the region between the Fichtel Mountains[278] and the Danube. It is evident from the visitation reports that, to a certain extent, pilgrimages did not come to an end and were nearly ineradicable, despite all prohibitions. Even 70 to 80 years after the Reformation was introduced and despite the decades-long, severe countermeasures of the Calvinistic government, the populace was still seeking out a large number of old pilgrimage sites within as well as without the territory of the Upper Palatinate. Likewise the converse: People from the neighboring lands of Bohemia and Bavaria also continued making pilgrimages into the now evangelical Upper Palatinate. The visitors of the great territorial visitations from 1579 to 1583 found that some miraculous images[279] had still been preserved and commanded that they be removed. Such commands simply were not carried out in some places.[280] Visitation reports from 1598–1600 and 1615ff. show that pilgrimages continued; in some places where shrines had meanwhile been destroyed, the number of pilgrims waned, but not always. Pilgrimage sites documented for 1615 were

---

[274] *Kurpfalz*—this is the County Palatine of the Rhine, the palatinate governed by one of the seven electors. – KGW

[275] Ernst Walter Zeeden, "Grundlagen und Wege der Konfessionsbildung," *Historische Zeitschrift* 185 (1958), 279 note 6.

[276] Sehling 5:195, 425. [The order does not specify what punishment, only that it is "requisite" (*unnachlessig*).]

[277] Zeeden (second note above this), 279.

[278] The Saale River flows northward and the Eger River flows eastward out of the Fichtel Mountains. – KGW

[279] *Gnadenbild* means "image of grace" and is also called a sacred image, an image of a saint reputed to work miracles, thus the goal of pilgrimages. – KGW

[280] For example in Pappenberg, Götz, *Wirren*, 55, 89, 105.

a) outside of the territory, yet sought out by people from the Upper Palatinate: Maria Kulm [in Egerland] and the fourteen helpers in time of need in Tachau and Frauenberg—all in Bohemia[281]; St. Salvator (Bettbrunn) near Ingolstadt [Bavaria], the pilgrimage church of St. Barbara on the Eixlberg near Nabburg in the Landgraviate of Leuchtenberg, among others;

b) within the land, of general significance: Cham, St. Lampert or Lamberg near Cham, Trautmannshofen, Pappenberg, Ammerthal;

c) within the land, but more of local significance: St. Bozo near Wurz, Söllnitz near Trausnitz, Schweibach near Albertshofen, St. Jobst near Tännesberg, Fahrenberg near Pleystein, Stadlern near Viechtach.

People went to the shrines and vowed to go there to counter illnesses, for example, of livestock, horses, children, (Schweibach, Frauenberg, Wurz), on account of certain ailments or infirmities (headaches, eye diseases: Tachau; sore arms and feet: Stadlern). Certain places were sought out on certain days; for example, Atzmannricht in the Prince-bishopric of Bamberg on Wolfgang's Day (October 31), or St. Lampert near Cham on Walpurgis' Day (May 1), where about 300 Bavarians flocked together in 1615 and came from distances of up to 70 miles.[282] Ten days later larger crowds from Cham made their pilgrimage to the same place—presumably because they lived according to the Julian calendar, meaning their May 1 came only ten days later. The visitors did not accept their excuse of having gone there to "enjoy" themselves. On the contrary, they suggested totally destroying the dilapidated little church and driving away the pilgrims with soldiers.[283] The custom of offering something to the shrines likewise continued unbroken; flax, black hens, wax, also money and other things were gladly offered. Aside from flax, for example, salt, grease, and eggs were also offered in Trausnitz; in

---

[281] These three cities are now in the Czech Republic: Chlum Svaté Maří, Tachov, and (presumably) Hluboká nad Vltavou. – KGW

[282] Zeeden says fifteen *Meilen*, but it is unclear which German *Meile*. Converting fifteen *Meilen* of 7500 meters into our miles of 5280 feet results in 69.9 miles. – KGW

[283] Götz, *Wirren*, 299f.

Trautmannshofen the pilgrims gave their offerings to the ill and beggars, who apparently also knew the date well and appeared before the church doors in great number.[284] Remarkably, it appears that the local evangelical parsons were also drawn into the rites of a pilgrimage. For example, the Trausnitz parson had to preach four times a year at the pilgrimage destination in Söllnitz near Trausnitz and was compensated for this from the incidental offerings; in Pappenberg, ever since the Mass was abolished, the evangelical parson read a "chapter" on the eve before the main pilgrimage day, and then the trip to make the offering took place. In 1615 the Calvinistic visitors proposed that the parson should no longer accept the offerings; from this one may infer that up until then he had been accepting them. Finally, it is worth pointing out that, even when the miraculous images were removed or the churches destroyed, pilgrimages did not come to an end. Indeed, the pilgrims entered the church when there was opportunity and bowed before the main altar and prayed before it.[285] In Trautmannshofen the council had the offering box demolished, in Pappenberg the miraculous image was burned, the interior of both churches on site in Ammerthal was cleared out; additionally, the church in Pappenberg and in Trautmannshofen was locked, and the pilgrimage church in Stadlern was destroyed. Nevertheless, these places received an influx of pilgrims and, in some form or another, offerings were given there.[286] We do not have the same level of detail for all the other territories as we do for the Upper Palatinate. In addition, this territory was surrounded by Catholic lands, thus many a custom may have received a little external support. All the same, here there is an example of the populace of a land, which had been led to Protestantism since about 1540, that held fast to old Catholic practices of making pilgrimages and venerating saints into the second decade of the seventeenth century, although the government continuously stepped in against this. Whoever was caught making a pilgrimage by an official of the Palatinate was punished. Nevertheless, the people continued to make

---

[284] Götz, *Wirren*, 346, 355.

[285] As in Cham, Götz, *Wirren*, 299; Nottarp, 19, has an isolated example of the evangelical populace of a Mazovian area having made such an annual pilgrimage to a Catholic church in the vicinity into the twentieth century.

[286] Götz, *Wirren*, 55, 88ff., 105ff., 238f., 275f., 199f., 345ff., 355.

pilgrimages (only for understandable reasons as inconspicuous as possible on the surface).[287]

While the church orders unanimously rejected visitation of shrines, they acted non-uniformly toward the pre-Reformation customs of bell tolling during storms and tolling the *Ave* bell. Tolling of the *Ave* bell, also called tolling for peace (*pro pace*), the Turks' bell, the *Angelus* bell, and *Salve* tolling, found approval in the majority of cases;[288] yet they did not agree on whether tolling should be two or three times a day, and if two times, whether it should be mornings and evenings,[289] or middays and evenings.[290] The great church order of Elector August of Saxony from 1580 even expressly complained that the tolling for peace had fallen out of practice in some places and impressed it anew, whereby it anticipated and met possible objections with the direction that one should not have exaggerated fear of the papacy, as if it would creep in again with the *Salve* tolling; moreover one should conceive of the tolling as a "reminder and incitement to proper, true, and Christian prayer."[291] On the other hand people did not share such views everywhere; elsewhere they may instead have held the opposite to be in order out of different pastoral convictions or perhaps even convictions no longer pastoral: Thus for Coburg 1554/55 in regard to the *Ave* and *Salve* tolling it was decreed that they should be stopped "for the sake of sojourning and neighboring people, so that they do not regard us as papistic."[292]

---

[287] Götz, *Wirren*, 347f.

[288] See excurses at the end of this chapter.

[289] 1569 Pomeranian church order, Sehling 4:399.

[290] Osterode in East Prussia, Sehling 4:151.

[291] Sehling 1:431.

[292] Sehling 1:544; similarly the 1552 ordinance for Reuss, Sehling 2:156. On the origin and significance of tolling to signal prayer time see Sehling 6/2:1047 note 27. [Zeeden's quote from the Coburg visitation ordinance should not be read as if the Marian practice had remained until that point. The concern was that people would hear the traditional threefold tolling and incorrectly assume that prayers were being offered to Mary: Not only "the three bell tolls mornings and evenings, which were called the *Ave Maria* and *salve* in the papacy," were to cease, but also tolling during storms (Sehling 1:544), which is addressed in the next paragraph. Zeeden's second reference here, 1552 Reuss, also addresses tolling during storms, but does not mention any Marian tolling. Instead it adds: "Tolling for the souls of all the faithful

The situation with tolling during storms was a little different. This must have been quite popular and enjoyed a great degree of respect.[293] For the most part it was forbidden, but that did not at all mean that it was not actually done. Several orders retained it, as the highly

---

[departed] on Saturday must also be abrogated, for it is offensive and reeks of the papacy" (Sehling 2:156). This practice is exemplified by an Austrian text from 1510, in which benefactors paid for the sexton to toll all bells "to comfort and aid the souls of all the faithful [departed]" every Saturday after Vespers while the priest went around the cemetery with a censer (Charter 10136 in the Stadtarchiv for Bludenz, in the Vorarlberger Landesarchiv, http://www.mom-ca.uni-koeln.de/mom/AT-VLA/BludenzStadtA/10136/charter). However, the 1570 Weimar *Generalia* may indicate a genuine remnant of Marian tradition there: "The idolatrous altars and images in the churches as well as all the superstitious *ave Maria, salve, pacem*, and tolling away the dead shall be prohibited and abolished" (Sehling 1:689).]

[293] George S. Tyack writes, "No theory of the beneficent power of bells was more wide-spread than the belief that they were a protection against lightning and storm. . . . Henry Bullinger seems to think that this idea arose from the people being summoned to prayer by the voice of the bell in time of any severe storm, and that afterwards the sound of the bell itself came to be counted efficacious in such cases. In the fifth of his 'Decades' (published in 1551) he says, 'About bells there is a wonderful superstition. They are christened by bishops, and it is thought that they have power to put away any great tempest. In the old time men were stirred up to prayer by the ringing of them, what time any sore tempest did rise; but now the very ringing of bells, by reason of their consecration, seemeth to have a peculiar kind of virtue in it' " (p. 211f. in *A Book About Bells*, London: William Andrews, 1898). Salt and water were blessed and then used to "wash" bells in a rite to consecrate them (benediction of bells). People commonly referred to the rite as the Baptism of bells due to the numerous similarities. Tyack (p. 80f.) gives translations of common Latin inscriptions on bells: "Lightning and thunder I break asunder" (*fulgura frango*), "The winds so fierce I doe disperse" (*dissipo ventos*), "the lightning's power break" (*fulmina frango*), "The lightning I shatter . . . The hurricanes scatter" (*fulgora frango . . . dissipo ventos*). The 1528 "Instructions for the Visitors of Parish Pastors in Electoral Saxony" allow for tolling during storms to continue as a call to prayer, but pastors are to give the people a clear explanation of its purpose, so that they do not adhere to their superstitious beliefs (*LW* 40:311f., *WA* 26:233 line 38 to 234 line 26, Sehling 1:170). Although not addressed by Zeeden, Tyack mentions another superstition associated with bell tolling: the power to scatter pestilence, as seen in the inscription "The plague I put to flight" (*pestem fugo*) (p. 81, 212f.). – KGW

conservative order from 1610 for St. Mary's church in Danzig, which strictly regulated the duties of the bell-ringers for tolling during storms along with their payment for doing so.[294] The conviction that lightning would not strike during a thunderstorm as far as the sound of the storm bell could be heard was so deeply and firmly ingrained in the urban and rural populace, which was at the mercy of the elements in a way entirely different from today, that it could not be shaken even by Reformation views to the contrary. In this point the Upper Palatinate once again offered a wealth of instructive examples. Since Ottheinrich's church order of 1556, the tolling during storms was forbidden along with other "idolatries." Mandates to refrain from it were declared periodically until the years right before the Thirty Years' War. Where the parsons or sextons did not do it, however, the peasants quite often became rebellious. The visitors from the year 1557 reported that the peasants forced the parsons to have the bells tolled; the visitors of the great visitation from 1579–83 heard from a squire that there would be a peasants' revolt if the tolling was not done; in another place, a village captain offered to ring the bells himself if the sexton would not do it; in yet another place the peasants forced the pastor himself to ring since the sexton had refused. From the popular views that manifested themselves with this we mention the following two: In Kümmersbruck people did not engage in long debates over worth or worthlessness at all; one time the bells were not rung and the storm destroyed everything. This lesson sufficed. And still in the year 1615 the visitors found that the storm bell of Perschen enjoyed special trust, since people were convinced that it could split the clouds of heaven.[295]

---

[294] Sehling 4:207.

[295] Götz, *Bewegung*, 136ff., 154; *Wirren*, 60, 106, 239, 273ff., 348, 355. [George S. Tyack gives a later example from which one would expect the opposite conclusion concerning the effectiveness of this practice: When a severe storm broke out over Brittany in 1718, the twenty-four churches whose bells were ringing were struck by lightning, while none of the churches whose bells were not tolled was struck (*A Book About Bells*, London: William Andrews, 1898) p. 213.]

TRANSLATOR'S EXCURSUS ON THE *AVE* BELL, TURKS' BELL, THE *ANGELUS* BELL, AND *SALVE* TOLLING

Although these are not all identical, they overlap; for Lutherans, of course, their Marian aspects were intolerable. *Salve* tolling was associated with the *Salve regina* (see note 249 above). The daily practice of tolling the *Ave* bell or *Angelus* bell in the morning, at noon, and in the evening began in the sixteenth century, although the evening tolling began three centuries earlier. It called Catholics to pray several brief texts, the first beginning with *"Angelus Domini nuntiavit Mariae"* (The angel of the Lord declared unto Mary), interspersed three times with the *"Ave Maria"* ("Hail Mary," based on the angel Gabriel's greeting in Luke 1:28; cf. *Liber Usualis* p. 1861). Lutherans who retained the tolling of these bells dropped the Marian prayers as being contrary to God's Word and against the will of Mary. Instead, they prayed the Lord's Prayer and prayers for peace, good government, the needs of body and soul of friend and foe, etc. In effect, it became their practice of tolling for peace. See, for example, the 1529 Hamburg church order (Sehling 5:513) and the 1569 Braunschweig-Wolfenbüttel church order (Sehling 6/1:180). The latter adds that the children may sing *Erhalt' uns Herr bei deinem Wort*, a hymn of Luther presumably written in 1541 (*WA* 35:235–248, 467f., "Lord, Keep Us Steadfast in Your Word," *LSB* 655), and *Verleih' uns Frieden gnädiglich*, a hymn of Luther from 1529 based on an antiphon *pro pace* (*Da pacem Domine*, see note 58 above).

The 1528 "Instructions for the Visitors of Parish Pastors in Electoral Saxony" not only speak to Marian associations with tolling for peace (*LW* 40:312f., *WA* 26:234 line 27 to 235 line 5, Sehling 1:171), but also have a section addressing the threat of the Turk, which concludes by instructing preachers to exhort the people to pray for protection from the Turks and explain that fighting them by the command of authorities is a true service to God (*LW* 40:306, *WA* 26:229 line 44ff., Sehling 1:168). When the Turkish army laid siege to Vienna in 1529 and again threatened to take it in 1541, the Turks' bell was rung daily at noon to call people to pray for peace against the Turk, i.e., the Ottoman Empire. "According to tradition," however, the origin of this practice goes back to a decree of Pope John XXII in 1322, in which he ordered the antiphon *Da pacem* to be prayed three times when the Turks' bell tolled (p. 242 of *Die biblischen Quellen der Lieder* by Rudolf Köhler, Vol. 1 Part 2 of *Handbuch zum Evangelischen Kirchengesangbuch*, ed. by Mahrenholz and Söhngen, Göttingen: Vandenhoeck & Ruprecht, 1965). In 1456, Pope Callixtus III ordered the Lord's Prayer and Hail Mary each to be prayed three times when the Turks' bell tolled to help the Hungarians defeat the Turkish army, a practice that continued even after the battle was won. This bull was not the first document to associate the Hail Mary with tolling for peace, but it was different in that it granted a forty-day indulgence to those who prayed accordingly once, and a hundred-day indulgence to those who did so three times while kneeling (p. 20 of *Die Türkenbulle Pabst Calixtus III: Ein deutscher Druck von 1456 in der ersten Gutenbergtype*, ed. by Paul Schwenke, Berlin: M. Breslauer, 1911). For examples of the Lutheran practice, see the 1542 church order for the Barony of Seidenberg (Sehling 3:366, see also 375, 444) and the 1543 Braunschweig-Wolfenbüttel church order, which has tolling every day at noon to pray for peace, good government, and the upper hand against enemies, such as the Turk. Pastors were to exhort the people to do this upon hearing the bell, whether in their house, yard, or field. It also says that children and others can "sing for everlasting peace against the pope and the Turk with a short hymn, as is now the custom among us" (Sehling 6/1:71). This is a reference to Luther's hymn *Erhalt' uns Herr bei deinem Wort*, which included the line "Restrain the murderous Pope and Turk." The order adds that, if desired, people in the church can sing the hymn for peace *Verleih' uns Frieden gnädiglich*. See also Graff 1:226f. and the 1541 "Appeal for Prayer Against the Turks" (*LW* 43:213–241, *WA* 51:585–625).

Not all tolling for peace was associated with the Turks. Heinrich Otte supplies an excerpt from 1446 explaining the practice of tolling *pro pace* with three sets of three peals: "those who pray the Lord's Prayer once and the Hail Mary three times for the peace and unity of the Church when the bell tolls *pro pace* mornings and evenings," etc., and mentions two theories for how this practice originated: at either the beginning or end of the thirteenth century, with Pope Innocent III's alteration of the Agnus Dei or with Pope Nicholas III's insertion of a prayer for peace before the Agnus Dei, respectively (p. 36 of *Glockenkunde*, 2nd ed., Leipzig: Weigel, 1884). Examples of separate prayers for peace and against the Turk are found in the 1580 Mansfeld agenda (Sehling 2:231f.).

Another example shows the value of knowing when the Reformation was introduced in a place before assuming that a document's condemnation of a practice meant that it had survived among Lutherans there for some years: The 1537 visitation articles for the pastors and preachers in Freiberg (Duchy of Saxony) say that the *Ave Maria* should no longer be tolled, due to abuse, and that all chants invoking saints, such as the *Salve regina* and *Regina caeli*, are to be abrogated from that time on (Sehling 1:466, printed as 646). Those articles are not marked with day and month, but Duke Heinrich's instructions for the visitors are dated May 26, 1537 (Sehling 1:460), the day before the divine service introducing the Reformation to the city (p. 392 of the entry "Heinrich der Fromme" in *Neue deutsche Biographie*, Vol. 8, Berlin: Duncker & Humblot, 1969). The 1538 visitation articles say that the tolling for peace can be reinitiated for its intended purpose (Sehling 1:468). Incidentally, this was the only point over which the duke expressed concern when ratifying the articles (Sehling 1:460). – KGW

CHAPTER 2

LEGAL AND ECONOMIC CONDITIONS

I. TRADITIONS IN ECCLESIASTICAL LAW

Whenever complications not bound to any particular confession or sovereignty intervened—which was more often the case in the west and southwest, but more the exception in the north and east—then the old organization of parishes with their out-parishes, endowments, fiefs, prebends, and competences[296] usually remained intact; likewise with their aggregation according to deaneries and their subordination to a higher ecclesiastical jurisdiction. The right of patronage (*ius patronatus*) and the right of collation transferred over from Catholic into evangelical church law without special changes.[297] And even if

---

[296] An out-parish did not have its own parson and was affiliated with a mother parish. A competence was an income sufficient to live on modestly. A prebend had various forms and could also be called a benefice; it was generally the income a canon or chapter member received from the revenue of an estate or land (also called a prebend) belonging to his cathedral or collegiate church. An ecclesiastical fief could be church estate granted to a secular person by feudal tenure or a benefice. Benefices involved the right of patronage and the right of collation, explained in the following note. See also "Fief, Ecclesiastical" in *The New Schaff-Herzog Encyclopedia of Religious Knowledge*, vol. 4, p. 310 (ed. by Samuel M. Jackson, Grand Rapids: Baker Book House, 1952), and "collation," "benefice," and "prebend" in *The Law of the Church: A Cyclopedia of Canon Law for English-Speaking Countries*, by Ethelred Taunton (London: Kegan Paul, Trench, Trübner & Co., 1906). – KGW

[297] The right of patronage refers primarily to a patron's right to propose a clergyman to someone with the right of collation, generally a bishop, in order to fill a vacant benefice (the right of presentation; collation is the

some things in matters of matrimonial law were altered for dogmatic reasons, the matrimonial jurisdiction remained reserved for the ecclesiastical court as before. It was already recalled above that the practice of evangelical marriage knew of the binding engagement as well as the forbidden degrees and closed times.[298] Even the Lutheran churches, after a period of initial hesitation, returned to administration of the greater ban, that is, solemn excommunication. The early church orders were content with the so-called lesser ban (*suspensio a sacris* [suspension from the holy things]). It excluded congregation members who lived in grievous sins like divorce and gluttony, or had committed crimes, from partaking of the Lord's Supper and from being godparents, insofar as a preceding pastoral admonition had not born fruit and so long as those concerned showed no contrition. This was also the view of the Lutheran Confessions, for example the Apology and the Smalcald Articles.[299] Even as the Smalcald Articles,

---

appointment of a clergyman to a benefice). See, for example, "Patron and Patronage" in *The Catholic Encyclopedia* vol. 11 (Johannes Baptist Sägmüller, New York: Robert Appleton Company, 1911). "The patronage of a church built on a lord's territory belonged to him as a matter of course, unless he had expressly granted the right to the individual or congregation that built it. The Reformation took over patronage along with the parish. Calvinism rejected it with lay control over the church as a whole. The Evangelical church ordinances in so far as they dealt with patronage fell in more or less with canon law. Conservatism with reference to patronage made itself evident in that, after the Peace of Westphalia, Roman Catholics were permitted to exercise the right of patronage over Protestant churches, and vice versa. The absorption of cloistral estates led frequently to an increase of patronage; the princes not only securing the patronage of monasteries, but all inherent rights over churches incorporated with them. The decline of episcopal jurisdiction not being always immediately succeeded by a strict consistorial government also favored an increase of patronage." *The New Schaff-Herzog Encyclopedia of Religious Knowledge*, vol. 8, p. 390 (ed. by Samuel M. Jackson, Grand Rapids: Baker Book House, 1953). A study dealing with the right of patronage in German lands in the fifteenth and sixteenth centuries is *Territorialstaat und Kirchenregiment. Studien zur Rechtsdogmatik des Kirchenpatronatrechts im 15. und 16. Jahrhundert* by Jörn Sieglerschmidt (Köln: Böhlau, 1987). – KGW

[298] See the paragraph after note 195 above.

[299] *BSLK*, 400, 456 and elsewhere; a compilation of the church orders concerned is in Wilken, 34f.; among others, these included: 1528 Braunschweig (Sehling 6/1); 1536 Hannover (Sehling 6/2); 1535 Pomerania (Sehling 4); 1540 Mecklenburg, 1529 Hamburg, 1531 Lübeck (Sehling 5).

so also the Wolfenbüttel church order of 1543 repudiated the greater ban as a papistic abuse, and relegated it to the domain of secular authority.[300] In the second half of the sixteenth century, however, the greater ban appears to have become accepted contrary to the views of the confessions.[301] The 1584 Prussian church order distinguished from the "milder castigation of penance imposed by the church" (the lesser ban) the "most extreme and most severe remedy of the [greater] ban."[302] Stated oversimply and most generally, this referred to the infliction of civil penalties or punishments for spiritual failings, or an ecclesiastical punishment with civil consequences. The punishment of

---

[300] Sehling 6/1:67: "For the greater ban, upon which the pope and priests have encroached, belongs simply to the secular authorities" [the word for "priests" here is *papen*, Low German for *Pfaffen*]; Smalcald Articles III, ix: *BSLK*, 456f.: The greater excommunication, which the pope retains, we regard only as a civil penalty, and it does not concern us ministers of the Church. (*Majorem illam excommunicationem, quam papa retinet, non nisi civilem poenam esse ducimus non pertinentem ad nos ministros ecclesiae*) [this is followed by a brief explanation of the lesser excommunication].

[301] Commenting on Smalcald Articles III, ix, Edmund Schlink says, "This statement seems to be contradicted by Luther's demand in the Preface to the Small Catechism regarding excommunicated persons 'that parents and employers should refuse to furnish them with food and drink' and 'that the prince is disposed to banish such rude people from his land' (S.C. Pref., 17). But this measure is not to be understood as a measure of the spiritual office but of the civil ... " and notes that the distinction between the greater (secular) ban and the lesser (ecclesiastical) ban "must not be confused with a differentiation between the greater and the lesser excommunication *within* the discipline of the church" (emphasis original, p. 212 in *Theology of the Lutheran Confessions*, trans. by Paul Koehneke and Herbert Bouman, Philadelphia: Muhlenberg Press, 1961). Schlink then points us to A. F. C. Vilmar's discussion of this in *Von der christlichen Kirchenzucht: Ein Beitrag zur Pastoraltheologie* (Marburg: Elwert, 1872), 57ff. Vilmar describes the lesser ban as a temporary exclusion from the Lord's Supper; any pastor can enforce this. The greater ban, the anathema, he describes as cessation of all pastoral care, participation in public services and the sacraments, churchly benefits and privileges of an external nature, and close associations with church members; this can be proclaimed only by the higher church authorities (the consistory). Secular consequences are not a part of this greater ban, but may occur on account of secular authorities who are Christian. Vilmar emphasizes that the Church is concerned with retention of sins and exclusion from the churchly community, not civil penalties. – KGW

[302] Sehling 4:131. [The bracketed insertion is from Zeeden.]

the greater ban became operative whenever someone initially put under the lesser ban did not react to another admonition (this time from the consistory) or being summoned before the consistory achieved no result. The biblical foundation for the solemn expulsion included passages such as Deuteronomy 13 and 17; Matt. 7, 16, and 18; John 16 and 20; Acts 5, 8, and 13; 1 Cor. 5; 2 Cor. 12 and 13; Gal. 6; 1 Tim. 5; Titus 3; and 2 Thess. 5.[303] At the same time some church orders appealed to the example of the Church Fathers and apostrophized the "old canons."[304] The authority to pronounce excommunication rested with the consistory, which here, as so often, embraced the spirit and substance of the old episcopal jurisdiction. Often the church orders expressly stated that excommunication was not something to which the parsons were entitled.[305] While the 1579 visitation decree for Salzwedel [in the Old Mark] emphasized that the elector of Brandenburg rejected the greater ban with the estates of the Augsburg Confession—which, however, did not prevent the Kölln-Berlin consistory from observing it—, the Mansfeld consistorial order of 1586 expressly appealed to Luther and Melanchthon in its tenth chapter ("On the Christian ban and ecclesiastical punishment") with its injunction not to despise the ban and its distinction between the greater and the lesser ban, quite in contrast to the Apology and Smalcald Articles: "Therefore, since the ancients also used to separate the ban with particular weighty reasons, and to distinguish between the lesser and the greater excommunication, a distinction that the beloved man of God Dr. Luther, Mr. Philipp Melanchthon, and other distinguished teachers hold in high regard and use in our time as well; this distinction shall be retained not only on account of the example of these excellent men, but also on account of other weighty reasons."[306] The greater ban applied to publicly revealed criminal offenses, vices, and transgressions against the faith, under which the following were subsumed without finer distinction: godlessness, papism, sectarianism, fanaticism, witchcraft, superstition, and

---

[303] Cf. the 1585 Lauenburg church order, Sehling 5:447–456.

[304] 1585 Lauenburg, Sehling 5:449, 457.

[305] For example the 1584 Prussian church order, Sehling 4:130f.; 1579 Salzwedel, Sehling 3:275; 1585 Mansfeld, Sehling 5:450.

[306] Sehling 2:209f.; the Lauenburg church order, Sehling 5:458: Luther restored the "right and proper use" of the "binding key."

contempt for the ruling doctrine.[307] The procedure itself consisted in that, following a respective judgment of the consistory, the person to be solemnly excommunicated was to be led into the church on a Sunday and the local clergyman read the excommunication formula over him in front of the assembled congregation. Subsequently the sexton (sacristan) was to lead him out of the church. Moreover, the excommunicant was to listen diligently to the preaching service. The 1569 Wolfenbüttel church order appointed "a separate seat in the church where the excommunicated person should stand every Sunday and festival at the time of the sermon."[308] If Communion was held, he had to leave the church before it began. The exclusion happened with respect to the church as a community of Christians and by virtue of the disciplinary authority, which the church possessed by divine right (*iuris divini*). The 1569 Wolfenbüttel church order adduced the following points of view as predominant in this: First, that not only the secular, but also the "ecclesiastical punishment" is "commanded to be used and executed by divine mandate and institution" against evil sinners and criminals; second, that it is commanded under a socio-ethical aspect, "so that a whole herd is not ruined by one bad sheep and the evil vexing example does not hurt and harm the common Christian assembly, also so that God's wrath and punishment may be avoided"; third, that (as the parsons should instruct their congregations "at the proper time") orderly and regular excommunication has to do with "a privation of all temporal and eternal welfare," even as, on the other hand, "the communion and community of the holy Christian Church is a community of all divine, heavenly goods."[309] In accordance with this, the excommunicant was regarded as "a severed member of the holy Christian Church."[310] The church orders occasionally recalled the seriousness of such a status with strong words; the Lauenburg church order of 1585 said of this, "that no greater affliction, danger, burden, and punishment could befall a man in his life on earth"; and the Mecklenburg consistorial

---

[307] Cf. for example the crimes to be punished by the consistory in the 1570 Kurland church order, Sehling 5:81f. [Instead of "the ruling doctrine," the church order says, "our doctrine and religion."]
[308] Sehling 6/1:207.
[309] Sehling 6/1:205, 206, 208.
[310] 1569 Wolfenbüttel, Sehling 6/1:208; likewise the 1570 Mecklenburg consistorial order, Sehling 4:246f.

order of 1570 drew up an excommunication formula deserving reproduction here in order to convey an impression of the severity, power, and dignity of the view of the disciplinary authority of the church which prevails here. According to it, on Sunday the pastor had to address the congregation from the pulpit in the presence of the person to be excommunicated as follows: "Dear friends ... " (some paragraphs about the ban and the offender follow here) "on account of which I, as the common servant and curate (*Seelsorger*) of this Christian Church, in the name of our Lord Jesus Christ, now hand over this unrepentant (corrupter, blasphemer, adulterer, fornicator, usurer), _name_, to the devil for the destruction of the flesh, that his spirit might be saved on the day of the Lord, should he turn again. [I] hereby proclaim God's terrible wrath and displeasure, and that he shall be shut out and cut off from any communion with all saints in heaven and on earth, and cursed and eternally damned with all devils in hell, as long as he persists in this impenitence."[311] In several lands—for example in the duchies of Lauenburg and Braunschweig-Wolfenbüttel—an official, magistrate, bailiff, "or lord and authority of the place" had to announce the civil consequences to someone excommunicated in this way; they consisted in the prohibition of taking part in weddings, "festivities and honorable society." At the same time, members of the congregation were prohibited by severe punishment from interacting with the excommunicant; in Mecklenburg and Kurland they were not even allowed to greet him "on the street or elsewhere" (of course with a pastoral-pedagogical goal, "so that he will be shamed and humbled and acknowledge his sins all the sooner and turn to God ... "). In matters of business transactions, to the extent that they are inevitable for continuing to live, a certain level of coexistence was of course unavoidable and also permissible in selling and buying, working in the forest and in the field, etc. Only one relatively early order believed that all association should be severed even in these basic matters.[312] Supervision over orderly execution of ecclesiastical punishment and the excommunicant's submission to it was likewise incumbent upon the local secular government; and if the excommunicant were not to

---

[311] Sehling 5:450, 245f. The same formula in Low German in Schleswig-Holstein, Feddersen, 522f.

[312] Prussia 1544, Sehling 4:68, repeated in the 1568 church order, Sehling 4:97f.

behave properly, secular punishments threatened him, which were sometimes specified, such as jail or exile.[313] Penitent excommunicants had to be reconciled publicly before the congregation in order to be received again into the churchly community, since they had been publicly excommunicated. They had to kneel down in the church in view of the congregation while the parson pronounced for them the formula of public confession and absolution, and subsequently readmitted them to the Lord's Supper. Whoever died under excommunication was denied a Christian burial. He was to be buried outside of the church cemetery without participation of the congregation, or at most in the presence of some family and friends, "without any Christian ceremonies, singing, and bell tolls, in complete silence, and to the horror of others."[314]

If the greater and lesser bans were largely in practice, it surely presented an exception when a prince acting as chief bishop (*Summepiscopus*, or *summus episcopus*) imposed the interdict over a whole parish, incidentally, on account of insufficient church offerings. This was issued in the name of Duke Friedrich III of Holstein-Gottorf on February 1, 1656 over the little city of Oldenburg in Holstein with the lovely rationale that, "as has been customary (!) up till now, action should be taken against the delinquents according to church law"; the same measure was repeated yet again seven years later, this time by the duke's successor, Christian Albrecht, the founder of the University of Kiel, because conditions had not improved in the meantime.[315]

Aside from this, appointing secular punishments for religious offenses was also an everyday occurrence in Protestantism. The

---

[313] The 1569 Pomeranian church order, Sehling 4:456; the Mansfeld consistorial order of 1586: Impenitents receive the command to leave the county within one month's time; if they do not achieve this, they are to be locked up and then sent across the border by means of the executioner, Sehling 2:210. [Zeeden does not further discuss the executioner, whose place in society at this time may interest the reader. See *Defiled Trades and Social Outcasts: Honor and Ritual Pollution in Early Modern Germany* by Kathy Stuart (New York: Cambridge University Press, 1999).]

[314] Lauenburg 1585, Sehling 5:454; with fewer directions, the Mecklenburg consistorial order of 1570, Sehling 5:246f., Wolfenbüttel 1569, Sehling 6/1:207f. Concerning the whole section on excommunication see also Feddersen, 521–524.

[315] Feddersen, 520.

church orders consistently approved of fines and prescribed them; in the case of more frequent repeat offenses, they prescribed punishments to dishonor the offender or even corporal punishments for failing to attend church, desecrating a festival, disrupting a service, and the like. Within Lutheranism in general people believed that there was no need to refrain totally from either Roman or canon law. Recourse to the imperial "common" or old ecclesiastical law, mostly with direct quotation from the book or canon concerned, is often encountered in the church orders; this is very frequently the case in sections on matrimonial law and forbidden degrees, but also for justifying the clergymen's salary in return for their care of souls (*cura animarum*).[316] Even where a canon law was not expressly named, it still found analogous application in many cases.[317] According to the 1567 consistorial order for the Bishopric of Schwerin, the old canons were not to be adduced only in those places where they stood in opposition "with divine Scripture." In cases of doubt concerning matters of matrimonial law they were to be tested against Holy Scripture, against Luther's writings on the subject, and against Melanchthon's "opinion in the theological examination entitled On Marriage."[318] Aside from that, however, they were to be applied so long as there was nothing objectionable on the part of divine and natural law. For matrimonial matters, book four of the Decretals was recommended.[319] The principle of application looked similar also in other church orders, such as in the Mecklenburg consistorial order of 1570. The Lauenburg order of 1585 continuously presupposed the canons, failed to follow them only where reservations arose in light of

---

[316] For example the 1585 Lauenburg church order, Sehling 5:412.

[317] Cf. Eugen Wohlhaupter, review of Feddersen in *Zeitschrift der Savigny-Stiftung für Rechtsgeschichte: kanonistische Abteilung* 59 [28] (1939), 665–676.

[318] For an overview of this subject from the sixteenth century view of Roman Catholicism, Luther, and other Lutheran reformers, see "The Reformation of Marriage Law in Martin Luther's Germany: Its Significance Then and Now," by John Witte, Jr. (*Journal of Law and Religion* 4.2 (1986): 293–351). For the writing of Melanchthon referred to by the order, see Appendix 1 in *The Chief Theological Topics: Loci Praecipui Theologici 1559*, trans. by J. A. O. Preus (St. Louis: Concordia Publishing House, 2011). – KGW

[319] Sehling 5:321f. [The Decretals is a collection of papal decretals in five books issued by Gregory IX in 1234.]

the Bible, and occasionally reduced their severity.[320] Greifswald taught canon law throughout the entire sixteenth century, namely the *liber sextus*.[321]

Furthermore in Silesia, more than once a jurisdiction of *Catholic* bishops survived within the evangelical territorial churches. Until the Council of Trent concluded (1563), the city of Breslau acknowledged an attenuated spiritual authority of the Breslau bishop. The Liegnitz superintendents acknowledged his right to ordination and still in 1592 regarded him as a secondary authority in matters of ecclesiastical law. The evangelical church conventions in the Barony of Pless regarded the bishops of Cracow and Breslau as proper authorities for their jurisdiction, likewise the parson Elogius in Habelschwerdt with respect to the archbishop of Prague.[322]

Publication of writings was under control of censorship. Even within Lutheranism, people believed they were not allowed to do without the imprimatur.[323] Despite the doctrine of the universal priesthood and despite all challenges to the existence of an essential difference between clergy and laity, the Lutheran clergy not only remained a separate class, but also retained their old, separate legal venue, at least as far as the privilege of the forum (*privilegium fori*) and the privilege of tax exemption were concerned. The church orders substantiated the special legal rights with the indication that for good reason it had been like this already for ages. Similarly they had the privilege of baking, milling, and brewing for their own needs.

---

[320] Sehling 5:236, 441.

[321] Plantiko, 135. [The *liber sextus* is "the sixth book," a collection of decretals issued by Boniface VIII in 1298 and so called because it supplemented the five promulgated by Gregory IX.]

[322] Sehling 3:391, 393, 454, 475.

[323] From the abundant examples I single out the 1587 visitation decree for Sondershausen, Sehling 2:127; the Mansfeld consistorial order of 1586, Sehling 2:200f. [The imprimatur referred to in the Sondershausen document is the approval of the superintendent (Sondershausen was part of the Lower County of Schwarzburg in Thuringia and a protectorate of Albertine Saxony). The Mansfeld order says that the consistory is responsible for inspecting publications to see that they glorify God alone, promote the truth, and cannot be misused for any sectarianism, frivolity, or other harmful purposes.]

II. ECONOMIC BASES OF THE PASTORATE (*PFARRBERUF*)

REVENUES AND AVOCATIONS OF CLERGY

Evangelical parsons generally drew their income from exactly the same sources as pre-Reformation clergy: from tithes, endowments, stole fees,[324] and special fees according to seasons and local customs. For the most part, secular authorities laid the greatest value on having nothing change in these matters and preserved church property by all available means and most vigorously. Under threat of punishment they demanded restoration of stolen church property and especially kept a close watch on the nobility, so that they would not appropriate church property on impulse—just as they in turn also had their magistrates watched, so that farmers at work tilling land would not encroach on glebes by plowing away a couple strips of land. Complaints about poorly maintained churches, half-dilapidated parsonages, neglected cemeteries, insufficient tithing, and peasants unwilling to pay were lacking in post-Reformation Lutheranism just as little as in pre-Reformation Catholicism. There was also no essential change to the distribution of expenses for constructing and maintaining buildings among patron, congregation, and parson. The stole fees continued, as did the fees in kind for certain occasions— even the age-old customary "offering" at funerals and at the churching of women after childbirth, indeed, even at pilgrimages, which were in principle forbidden. The circle of people who shared in these special revenues likewise remained about the same: Parson and vicar retained their old claims, but also sacristan, cantor, teacher, and choir members (schoolboys) had a right to what was traditionally found to be commensurate for churchly services rendered, for example, at weddings or high feasts. The chapter "On the Incidental Fees (*Accidentibus*)" took up a lot of space in not a few church orders.[325]

Even as many things remained as before in matters of law and custom, so also there was often little change in the various charges to which the pastoral estate (*Pfarrstand*) of the outgoing Middle Ages was liable. The social and economic dependency, especially of the

---

[324] *Stolgebühren*, also called surplice fees, are perquisites, fees paid to clergy for special services. – KGW

[325] These matters are always being regulated in the church orders, so I may refrain from providing individual references.

country clergy on nobility patrons, was a source of many evils already in the Middle Ages and by no means always had a favorable effect following the Reformation. Simoniacal conferment of parishes, extortion of money, and expropriation of land were cause for complaint in Brandenburg and Pomerania, but also elsewhere people liked to take something from the clergy when they entered office. In the Upper Palatinate, for example, people demanded of them money for taking possession of the benefice and various fees for the installation; here, however, the usufructuaries were officials or the state chancellery, and not so much the squires as in northern Germany. In Pomerania, however, the dominating position of aristocratic landowners gave rise to all sorts of further disadvantages. According to local custom in another place, the parson was occasionally entitled to brew and mill as well as to hunt—to "engage in hunting ... at the usual time ... for his remuneration (*ergetzlichkeit*)."[326] In Pomerania, in contrast, they had to be at the disposal of their squires and patrons as hunting servants and game drivers and be ready to render other more menial services, for example, as messengers and clerks. Therefore the landowners probably deliberately filled the offices of their parishes with less-cultivated people (incidentally without even asking the consistory), continued hunting, and elevated people to be pastors at will, which gave currency to the saying that one could "get priests (*Pfaffen*) more easily than cowherds."[327] When the Pomeranian church order of 1535 declared it unreasonable for the village parsons to tend sheep, cattle, and pigs in turn with the peasants, and the Prussian church order of 1540 expressly exempted clergy from precisely this tending duty in villages having no herders, it is easy to suppose that this exemption and these caveats were not grabbed from thin air. The fact that parsons were drawn in for tending duty if necessary was not so farfetched from the village and peasant perspective, since in the extensive agrarian territories of northern Germany the clergy, as far as circumstances allowed, were forced into farming anyway, presumably

---

[326] Zahna 1533, Sehling 1:716. [Zahna is northeast of Wittenberg in the electoral district of Saxony. The word "*ergetzlichkeit*" could mean "delight, pleasure, amusement" as well as "remuneration, recompense, reward," among other things.]

[327] Plantiko, 128ff.

just as their predecessors in the Catholic period were.[328] The Pomeranian church order of 1569 candidly verified that many parsons and preachers were so overwhelmed with their extensive farming that not only were they unable to study, but even in emergencies people were not able to find them at home, because they were roving about their fields or elsewhere. In Mecklenburg, where similar economic conditions prevailed, the pastors had to be admonished in the 1540/45 and 1552 church orders not to run into the field, at least not on Saturdays, which was prevalent, but rather to reserve this day for their spiritual vocation and to be in church in the afternoon for confession and Vespers.[329] Again, elsewhere it was not so welcome or a matter of course that the parson farmed with his own hands. In the Upper Palatinate, a thoroughly agricultural region, people complained if the parson himself went into the forest [to gather wood], used his own hands to load manure or work an oven, led oxen over the field, or stood in manure with bare legs—all of which happened, but by no means found the approval of the villagers there.[330] On the other hand, the inhabitants of the Upper Palatinate (and elsewhere, for that matter) regarded it as entirely appropriate and as a customary duty of country clergymen to keep for the congregation a bull and a boar for breeding in return for their small tithes[331] and Lenten fees—a custom which, by the way, many clergy groaned about as a heavy burden.[332]

---

[328] Sehling 4:336, 50; 1569 Pomeranian church order, Sehling 4:415.

[329] Sehling 4:336; 5:150, 201.

[330] Götz, *Wirren*, 49f., 314.

[331] With respect to plant life, the small tithe generally included things grown in gardens and cultivated with hoes and shovels as well as fruit and nuts (whereas the "great tithe" was cultivated with a plow and included corn and other grains as well as wine). With respect to animals, the small tithe generally included a tenth of newborn lambs, goats, calves, foals, piglets as well as chickens, ducks, and geese, bees, eggs, honey, and other animal products. See, for example, *DWB* "Zehnte" II, 1, a–b (vol. 31, col. 456f.) and "Zehnt" III, 2 in vol. 36, p. 499f. of *Theologische Realenzyklopädie* (ed. by Gerhard Krause, Gerhard Müller, Berlin: de Gruyter, 2004). Also refer to p. 41f. of "Luther's Pastors: The Reformation in the Ernestine Countryside" by Susan C. Karant-Nunn in *Transactions of the American Philosophical Society* vol. 69, part 8 (Philadelphia: The American Philosophical Society, 1979). – KGW

[332] Götz, *Wirren*, 48, 320; cf. also Friedrich Beyschlag, "Pfarrer als Zuchttierhalter," *Beiträge zur bayerischen Kirchengeschichte* 28 (1922), 15–24; for information about parsons as keepers of breeding animals in the

When pastors tilled their fields, as in northern Germany, it was often an extreme necessity: They had to be active beyond their spiritual vocation for their livelihood, which otherwise could not be sufficiently sustained.[333] The church order for Braunschweig-Wolfenbüttel issued in 1543 by order of the Smalcald League expressed the principle that clergy must be paid sufficiently, first since they did not have and were not allowed to have any auxiliary income (via craftsmanship or mercantile activities), and secondly since they were also not to collect any incidental fees for the administration of the Sacrament, the customary confessor's fee, and the like.[334] This ideal requirement succeeded only to a modest extent, however, and by far not everywhere. Instead, almost everywhere things stayed as before, as the farming of the pastors in northern Germany bore witness. Poor pay, an old affliction of the spiritual estate, had dragged itself also into the churches of the Reformation from the Middle Ages and, as before the Reformation, created a burden for exercising the office as well as for the reputation of the parsons and vicars with respect to their education and way of life. Of course, payment varied and was not always bad, just as it was not always bad before the Reformation. But then economic misery hardly constituted a rarity, and the methods for countering it likewise were not always new, rather quite traditional in many cases.[335] When a visitation decree for the city of Gollnow in Pomerania said that the wives of pastors and chaplains were permitted to brew and sell brandy because they had such a meager income, it speaks in clear language to

---

Archbishopric of Magdeburg, see Friedrich Hermann Otto Dannell, *Protokolle der ersten lutherischen General-Kirchen-Visitation im Erzstifte Magdeburg anno 1562–64* (Magdeburg: Selbstverlag des Herausgebers, 1864), vol. 1, p. 48 and vol. 3, p. 15. Occasionally, as in the diocesan estate of Waldsassen, parsons traditionally also had to provide for the hunting dogs of princes; in effect, the situation could often arise during hunting season where the parson would have to free up his own stalls for days for a pack of over thirty dogs and house his own livestock by a neighbor during this time; Götz, *Wirren*, 320.

[333] Cf. for example the 1552 Mecklenburg church order; the 1573 consistorial order of Brandenburg; the 1525 and 1540 Prussian church orders; the 1543 Wolfenbüttel church order. Sehling 5:217f.; 3:113, 119; 4:38, 49; 6/1:43.

[334] Sehling 6/1:43f.

[335] Cf. the material cited by Wilken, 43f.

the social state of clergymen there.[336] It was along the same line
elsewhere when underpaid chaplains were encouraged to reprieve
their existence with the help of auxiliary income: The chaplain of
Osterode in East Prussia gained his "civil nourishment" (*bürgerliche
Nahrung*)[337] in the city by managing a beer hall, though he received
instruction to keep himself "blameless"[338]—which, with the notorious
German propensity for drunkenness, was perhaps not always so easy
to carry out. In other cases it cannot readily be determined whether
need or greed drove the clergy, as in 1578 in Stendal, for example,
when they raised the "incidental fees" (*accidentalia*) five to
tenfold;[339] and when they "practiced the drink trade,"[340] that is,
managed a tavern or privately sold beer in the markets and little cities
of the Upper Palatinate, thereby creating competition for the
established citizens.[341] If the sale of beer and brandy was permitted or
even ordered in Pomerania and East Prussia, in Electoral
Brandenburg it was taboo. There the order of 1573 forbade parsons
from acting as "shopkeepers, merchants, or beer vendors." Various
visitation instructions also took very precise aim at the question of
secular avocations for the clergy when, among other things, they
inquired if he presumed to engage in medical or notarial activities, or
to practice profiteering.[342] According to the accusations of the Lübeck

---

[336] Sehling 4:509f.
[337] This is an old designation for a trade that could be pursued in a city by
right of one's citizenship there. – KGW
[338] Sehling 4:151.
[339] Sehling 3:331.
[340] As in Kurland, the 1570 church order, Sehling 5:112. [See p. 35ff. of B.
Ann Tlusty, *Bacchus and Civic Order: The Culture of Drink in Early
Modern Germany* (Charlottesville: University Press of Virginia, 2001) and
Alison Stewart, "Taverns in Nuremberg prints at the time of the German
Reformation," pp. 95–115 in *The World of the Tavern: Public Houses in
Early Modern Europe* (ed. by Beat Kümin, B. Ann Tlusty, Aldershot:
Ashgate, 2002). Neither of these, however, addresses the sale of alcohol by
clergy.]
[341] Götz, *Wirren*, 314.
[342] Sehling 2:423, 469; 5:431; Magdeburg 1583, Halberstadt 1588,
Lauenburg 1585; also Erfurt 1647 (visitation publication of the council):
Here the inquiry even extended to whether the pastor, when serving beer and
wine, availed himself of just or unjust measures, August Nebe "Der Erfurter
Landpastor im 17. Jahrhundert," *Zeitschrift des Vereins für*

council in 1582, it was less hazy whether need or greed formed the leitmotiv among the clergy there; the city government was convinced that the pastors were out for money when exacting occasional fees[343] and that, for example, they only preached at a funeral if the pastor had been included in the will. In the same sense, the Pomeranian synodical statutes of 1574 warned against pastors making demands for their own purposes under pretext of church ordinance.[344] Clearly it belonged in the category of allowable avocational activities when, alongside the chaplaincy, a chaplain filled the office of the town clerk, taught school, or operated the church clock.[345] By contrast, it was unusual when an order, as in Zittau in 1595, called it a traditional privilege of the parson along with the town clerk to use the cemetery as a pasture for his livestock. Other orders conceded to him (and the sacristan) the grass there, "or whatever else grows there," but did not allow him to bring his livestock onto the graveyard.[346]

With the matters just touched upon, we have already broached a broad and problematic topic, which we will continue in the following sections, though only in outline. By this I mean the continued existence of much-censured abuses within Protestantism, taken over from the late medieval church.

Kirchengeschichte der Provinz Sachsen und des Freistaates Anhalt 30 (1934), 21.
[343] Sehling 5:371f.
[344] Sehling 4:488. ["*praetextu ordinationis ecclesiasticae, in suos usus poscant*" (in Chapter 2, Section 27 of the *Statuta synodica in ecclesiis Pomeraniae*).]
[345] The 1563 parish order of Lassan in Pomerania, Sehling 4:516.
[346] Zittau 1595, Sehling 3:380; Halberstadt 1588, Sehling 2:472.

CHAPTER 3

CONTINUATION
OF CHURCHLY ABUSES

From the complex of questions and issues that have traditionally been grouped under the heading of churchly "abuses" and have commonly been brought up for interpreting the late Middle Ages, some subquestions shall be singled out in what follows. An exhaustive and adequate treatment is neither possible nor intended within the scope set for this book. We simply share some facts and accounts which indicate that the problem of abuses also occupied post-Reformation evangelical churches. Scholarly literature has long been deeply consumed with the morally and religiously contestable conduct of the pre-Reformation clergy. That in this point much lay in disorder is a fact that will not change. However, relatively few deliberations were made in prior research concerning how difficult it is to find the right standard for evaluation here; only recently has attention been drawn to this problem with greater emphasis.[347] In order to achieve a fair assessment, it will be necessary to bring the churchly abuses into view, first in connection with the economic and social conditions in which the clergy lived, and secondly in connection with the cultural standing of the clergy and the social class to which they belonged as well as the particular countryside (or city) in which they worked. Only after shedding light on these environmental conditions can a

---

[347] I refer especially to the latest publication of Oskar Vasella, *Reform und Reformation in der Schweiz. Zur Würdigung der Anfänge der Glaubenskrise.* (*Katholisches Leben und Kämpfen im Zeitalter der Glaubensspaltung* Heft 16), Münster in Westfalen: Aschendorff, 1958. [2nd ed., 1965.]

somewhat suitable judgment be formed. The same applies for the late Middle Ages as also for the clergy of all confessions in the age of the Reformation and Counter-Reformation.

What will be brought up in the following can be noted, therefore, with the proviso that the pertinent facts relating to the social situation, background, education, and environment must each be taken into account for the more deeply penetrating interpretation which we are not yet able to give here. Thus further-reaching conclusions may not be drawn immediately from the facts to be shared here. In part, it was a matter of isolated cases; in part, it concerned conditions that were bound to a particular city or countryside, or to the extent of a territory. Certainly some things recurred in scattered places, while others occurred independently of one another in many places. Here we may suppose that we are dealing with phenomena of a more general character.

Some material shall be presented in the following under the principal theme of what may have been passed on from the abuses and dubious customs of the Middle Ages: first, concerning the image of the parson; second, concerning the religious-moral degeneration of the congregations; and finally, concerning superstition, belief in magic, and the state of religious knowledge.

I. CONCERNING THE IMAGE OF CLERGY

The lifestyle, pastoral care (*Pastoration*), and educational level of late medieval clergy were open to criticism, but even among the evangelical clergymen after the Reformation they were not exemplary in places. Knowledge and education—if one can believe the complaints concerning these in the church orders, religion mandates, and visitation reports—also frequently left much to be desired. First, as far as what concerned education and background, the 1558 and 1573 Electoral Brandenburg church orders brought forth a great catalog of desires and complaints, which together constituted a vivid reflection of pastors, and from which we may selectively conclude that the patrons engaged in simony, presented [candidates] to parishes only in return for previously agreed upon concessions and in this way, in the language of the ordinance, made "inept and illiterate asses" into pastors.[348] The great visitation and consistorial order issued fifteen

---

[348] Sehling 3:93.

years later by Elector Johann Georg demanded of those possessing the right of presentation[349] that the candidates to be presented be "pious men who do not live in open vice" and who are well-versed in pure doctrine. He added that "tailors, cobblers, and other ruined tradesmen and idlers who have not studied their grammar, not to mention are unable to read properly, and who become priests (*Pfaffen*) of necessity, only because they have not properly tended to their occupation, are ruined, and find no escape, should not be permitted or received into such an important office, as has happened up till now."[350] People in Pomerania and Brandenburg complained particularly vehemently about pastors having come from the tradesman-class or other uneducated levels; such an ascent to the pastoral office (*Pfarramt*) was also not entirely precluded elsewhere, though the extent of its occurrence evades my knowledge. The relatively uniform surveys about the Upper Palatinate by J. B. Götz demonstrated that evangelical parsons in 1557 were to a large degree uneducated and "indolent," and were described by the visitors with such censures as "mediocre," "poorly taught," "responded badly," "did not know anything," "answered quite childishly."[351] As early as about 1580 only two of 320 parsons came from the tradesman-class, while 150 had attended a university. That did not, however, prevent the actual theological preparation from being moderately to poorly constituted, except for a fraction of these 320 parsons. In 1615 the education and conduct of Reformed parsons was designated as thoroughly proper. Thus a gradual improvement of the spiritual estate was unmistakable. The path to the pastoral office (*Pfarramt*) often took a circuitous route through the office of schoolmaster. Young men who had come from theological studies and viewed the school as a temporary position met here with tradesmen and people lacking a higher education, who likewise taught the youth and often also had a

---

[349] See the notes above at the beginning of Chapter 2. The order has a section entitled "On the calling and presenting of parsons," which begins as follows: "Although we have no desire to strip anyone of their old right to appoint church servants or the right of presenting and calling or nominating, we do want and admonish all the collators who have parishes to bestow to seek and present for this high office, on account of which the Son of God has shed His blood, as many capable people as possible, ..." (Sehling 3:107). – KGW
[350] Sehling 3:107.
[351] Götz, *Bewegung*, 143ff.

secondary (or primary?) vocation as sexton, additionally sometimes as clerk and civil servant.[352] In Brandenburg, instead of taking clergy from outside the electorate when there were applicants for a pastorate (*Pfarrstelle*), Elector Johann Georg even valued giving preference in case of doubt to Brandenburg schoolmasters and teaching assistants who lacked a higher education, since they were familiar with the local church customs.[353] On account of the particular liturgical situation in Electoral Brandenburg, this provision may not have been entirely incomprehensible, though it did indicate that the education of clergy at a university had by no means prevailed as an indispensable prerequisite (*conditio sine qua non*). Perhaps the same can be cautiously concluded as a conjecture based on the frequently recurring admonitions that a parson should study diligently, i.e. labor over his books, "distribute" his sermon "in several sections in a well-ordered fashion . . . and refrain from all frivolity and offensive speech and cursing from the pulpit,"[354] and also based on the regulations for the essentials of a parish library; in the rural communities of Electoral Brandenburg this quite understandably included the German and Latin Bible, Luther's House Postils,[355] and a copy of the church order.[356] The sermons were gladly drawn from the Postils, especially in the country. Many parsons simply read them from the pulpit.[357]

---

[352] Götz, *Wirren*, 38ff., 51, 321ff., 308–317.

[353] The visitation and consistorial order of 1573, Sehling 3:107. [This part of the order says that "parsons, chaplains, schoolmasters, and assistants should be called primarily from our university in Frankfurt an der Oder or, in the event of a shortage there, from other universities, schools, and churches that are beyond suspicion. If there also be any schoolmasters or teaching assistants in cities of our electorate who would let themselves be used for such offices, they should be considered and taken for this before others, in view of the fact that they know the church customs of our land and for that reason tend to become the most prominent people."]

[354] For example the 1573 Electoral Brandenburg church order, Sehling 3:112.

[355] *Sermons of Martin Luther: The House Postils*, trans. and ed. by Eugene F. A. Klug (Grand Rapids: Baker, 1996). – KGW

[356] As well as the visitation and consistorial order, Sehling 3:118. [The paragraph here lists the German Bible, but not the Latin Bible.]

[357] Pomerania: Plantiko, 128f.; Upper Palatinate: Götz, *Wirren*, 38ff., 59; normally, if not always, schoolmasters also did the same when they led the service in the stead of the absent clergyman; Götz, *Wirren*, 324. [For an excellent look at publication and use of postils in the sixteenth century, see

With the low level of education and knowledge, which Delius identified for the clergy in the subdistrict (*Amt*) of Querfurt between 1555 and 1583 from the visitation acts, supposedly the best they had to offer was still the reading of a chapter from Holy Scripture or a section from the Postils. It must not have been any different for the village pastors of Mecklenburg who engaged in agriculture.[358]

In matters of lifestyle and conduct, both of which may of course have a certain correlation with background and education, many church orders produced a series of demands; one cannot determine in detail the extent to which each of these demands was achieved or approached achievement, or to what extent they were utopian, unless comparison is made with visitation acts or comparable sources, insofar as such exist. The fact that church orders prohibited some things surely cannot be taken as certain proof that they all occurred; however a certain probability can be assumed, especially where the prohibitions took concrete and detailed forms rather than getting lost in generalities. Nevertheless, *loci communes* (commonplaces, common topics) were not always to be dismissed as mere expressions, as when it said in the 1558 church order for the villages of Brandenburg that a parson should not "go to the tavern for beer, but stay at home and study . . . also [he should] not have a beard or wear short clothes, but long and decent clothes, as his station requires," or as when a newly ordained clergyman, prior to his installation in a pastoral office (*Pfarramt*), had to subscribe (or else he would not be installed) to the declaration saying that he must refrain from drunkenness, gambling, and sitting around in bars, not to mention worse things.[359] Also taking into consideration that, according to the same Brandenburg consistorial order, the parsons were not to get

---

The Primacy of the Postils: Catholics, Protestants, and the Dissemination of Ideas in Early Modern Germany by John M. Frymire (Leiden: Brill, 2010). The issue of postils simply being read from the pulpit is addressed on pp. 77f., 82, 91–4, the House Postils being discussed on pp. 92–4. These pages show that postils were often published precisely with the intent of having country pastors read them from the pulpit, in part because of poor education, in part because they had to farm to earn a living. Although in 1535 Luther encouraged reading postils from the pulpit, in 1543 he expressed disappointment with doing so instead of independently studying and praying.]
[358] See the text following note 327 above; Delius, 81, 89.
[359] Sehling 3:91.

involved in foreign conflicts, be irascible, strike with a fist, or look for ways to make money (by usury, trade, or merchandizing), it is evident that matters were being touched upon that were by no means entirely theoretical.[360] The 1570 Kurland church order reported, for example, that alongside numerous pious and God-fearing pastors "in this crazy, vile world" there are unfortunately also "some, especially in the country," among whom "such an impious, wild life is led— unbecoming of any honest man in society (*im bürgerlichen Leben*)— with disorderly gorging, drinking, dancing, jumping, lewdness, and other wantonness of clothing," that no Christian can see it without being offended, not to mention that in light of such behavior the half-heathen natives would hardly have desire or cause to convert to true Christianity.[361] In the 1583 visitation report, likewise from Kurland, Duke Gotthard von Ketteler used stirring words to underscore the fears expressed in the church order above. He emphasized how, contrary to all expectations, "the occasional church visitations" had not effected any visible improvement and he, "not without heartache and pain," had to experience that the opposite of the intended was more likely to have occurred, namely, that one "gave too much freedom" to the parsons and did not curtail them, such that many of them permitted themselves extraordinarily evil conduct, beginning with hairstyle and clothing, and extending to riotous living—with hunting, shooting, and dancing—not to mention that they engaged more deeply in worldly matters, acted as procurators, traded, operated taverns, and "undertook even more indecent things of the sort"—and everything in direct opposition to the published church order.[362] It followed from visitations conducted elsewhere that, indeed, even the spiritual estate was not entirely free from some widespread vices. Assault, violence, and above all drunkenness, as well as avarice (less often, but definitely not isolated cases) repeatedly offered occasion for punishment and reproach. The visitation order for a village in the Mark made it clear to the pastor that he should not go into a tavern; if he did so anyway, later there would be no reason for him to wonder

---

[360] Sehling 3:112f.; cf. the numerous parallel examples in Wilken, 21f.: complaints of the church orders concerning the wicked living (*male vivere*) of clergy.
[361] Sehling 5:74.
[362] Sehling 5:112.

why the peasants gave him a thrashing.[363] In the Upper Palatinate between 1580 and 1615 it happened more than once, first, that the clergy themselves carried weapons, threatened to deal blows, lashed about themselves with their weapons, and even took their spear[364] or whatever else they had into the church with them; second, that they were mutilated: in one case by a chaplain, in numerous cases by people from the village.[365] As far as the drinking was concerned, which was complained of everywhere—Duke Bernhard's court preacher said in his funeral sermon for the duke of Weimar that the army chaplains had poured more glasses of wine down their throats [toasting] to His Princely Grace's health than the number of times they had prayed the Our Father for their lord[366]—there were extreme cases when it happened that before the sermon a pastor had already drunk one to three tankards of beer, or that, according to the 1582 complaint of the Lübeck council, "sometimes the ministers administered this venerable Sacrament laden with a good drink."[367] The avarice, in part quite naturally explicable by their being underpaid, usually designated as "greed" (Geiz)[368] in the church orders, unfortunately appeared to pass from the exception to the norm here and there (as in Lübeck, for example, according to the council's sharp critique) and otherwise bore bad fruit, insofar as they made

---

[363] Bagow 1553, Sehling 3:153. [Mark Brandenburg.]

[364] According to DWB "Spiesz" I, 1, b (vol. 16, col. 2438f.), it was an old German right that a free man could carry a spear for personal protection. – KGW

[365] Götz, Wirren, 44ff., 308ff.

[366] Albert Ludwig, Die evangelischen Pfarrer des badischen Oberlands im 16. und 17. Jahrhundert (Lahr: Schauenburg, 1934), 81.

[367] Götz, Wirren, 45; Sehling 5:372.

[368] Writing from the perspective of the Reformation, Hans Sachs published a dialog on precisely this topic in 1524: Ein Dialogus des inhalt ein argument der Römischen wider das Christlich heüflein; den Geytz, auch ander offenlich laster etc. betreffend (A Dialog Containing an Argument of the Romanists Against the Little Band of Christians; Concerning Greed and Other Manifest Vices etc.). In the preface to her 1970 edition of Sachs' prose dialogs, Ingeborg Spriewald notes that in those days, Geiz not only meant lust for money and possessions, but, like Wucher (usury), it was also a collective term for all kinds of deceptions based on self-interest, greediness, etc., for profit-seeking at all costs, without regard for charity and public welfare (Die Prosadialoge von Hans Sachs. Leipzig: VEB Bibliographisches Institut, 1970, p. 19, note 14). – KGW

pastoral care (*Seelsorge*) undesirable: The Brandenburg church order of 1540, for example, repudiated parsons' badgering the sick and dying to leave them something in their will, since this finally resulted in people no longer calling the clergy in such cases and abstaining from pastoral counsel.[369] On the other hand, it must have been an exception when the local parson played the shawm for the bridal couple from the tavern to the church and did the same on the way back after the wedding, in the end striking up music for dancing.[370]

II. ABUSES IN THE CONGREGATIONS

This negative image of the clergyman is complemented by approximately corresponding reports about the level of education and conduct of the congregations. For the idea that if the parsons degenerated, matters with the church members would not normally be much better, is not only an inference for which a certain probability speaks, but also a supposition born out by the church orders themselves in numerous provisions, not to mention the visitation acts. What we mention in the following are again only some examples that, like spotlights, illuminate the situation from a few select vantage points. These concern the degeneration of the church members, superstition, and lack of education.

A. DESECRATION OF FESTIVALS AND WORSHIP SPACE

Hundreds of church orders, territorial orders, council and policy mandates inculcated the hallowing of festivals till into the late seventeenth century. At the same time they described the common local and territorial forms of desecration and often immediately prescribed a punitive measure to match the offense. The common sight, met at every turn, was this: The people went for walks during the Sunday service—in the church, on the city wall, before the gate, and before the church in the cemetery (and there they engaged in "idle talk," if not also selling brandy[371]). The visitors of Elector Ottheinrich complained in 1557 that public carousing, dancing, and gambling went on unpunished "during the service," and to such an

---

[369] Sehling 5:372; 3:81.
[370] Götz, *Wirren*, 268.
[371] Magdeburg 1562; Sehling 2:409f., 412; municipal promulgation of Amberg in 1581 and report by Martin Schalling in 1578: Ramge 42ff., 133.

extent "that their punishment from God's Word is now a mockery."[372] That these things did not always go on quietly and unobtrusively is imaginable, and thus complaints are also directed at the great noise that happened along with these things. Almost stereotypically, complaints arose concerning the "people of Gomorrah" and the tavern business early on Sunday mornings; likewise concerning annual fairs being held on Sundays. Aside from amusements, working on Sundays and festivals drew complaints and critique, whether it was harvest work or woodwork, whether it was buying, selling, or loading, whether it was fishing, slaughtering, or some other manual labor.[373] In addition to this were the usual immoderations and excesses at christening feasts and celebrations for engagements and weddings.[374] It is no wonder, then, that church attendance and reception of the Lord's Supper suffered under such things; complaints were also made everywhere concerning poor regular church attendance on Sundays, as well as children and servants being absent from catechesis an inordinate amount. Nevertheless, the authorities sought with the greatest energy to check these conditions and countered them with numerous measures: They prohibited the selling of alcohol before noon, locked the gates and bars of doors, posted bailiffs, civil servants, and other controllers to monitor church and catechesis attendance, and imposed fines and imprisonment "so that," as the Pomeranian church order of 1569 formulated, "as much as possible, the common folk is induced to proceed from wildness to sanctification."[375] The effect of such regulations depended on the attention given to their enforcement, and this varied from region to region. Around 1580 in the Ernestine Duchy of Weimar well-ordered conditions prevailed, while at the same time in the neighboring subdistrict (*Amt*) of Querfurt, which belonged politically to the

---

[372] Götz, *Bewegung*, 152.

[373] Cf. the two previous notes; also Wilken, 42ff. with many examples.

[374] Material in Wilken, 46, 59, 61; particular cases (disgraceful conduct of the bride at the wedding, clamoring about in the church, fighting at the wedding reception) Wilkin, 61ff.

[375] See note 371 above; Wilken, 44, has numerous other quotes; this quote is from the 1569 Pomeranian church order, Sehling 4:386, originally in Low German.

Archbishopric of Magdeburg, many things were still topsy-turvy,[376] and the Lutheran visitors reported to the elector in Heidelberg that, in the Upper Palatinate, the desecration of Sunday had gained ground "in an unbelievable manner" and controlling it simply was not possible in some places since, for example, when the barkeepers were prohibited from selling during the service, the people ran across the border to nearby Egerland[377] and got for themselves there what was withheld from them at home on a festival.[378] Let us round off the illustration of this point with a powerful individual case: how Sundays and festivals were actually regarded in Wasungen, a parish in the County of Henneberg. A local clergyman (who had been ordered to report on the order of service observed in his congregation) provided his superintendent with an extremely clear and detailed account, which said, among other things: that many craftsmen went overland in order to peddle their wares at annual fairs; that the peasants worked and were not punished; in short, that the hallowing of festivals quickly went downhill and that, in his opinion, these were no small sins and disgraces for "us evangelicals," "that we have six days for work and making a living, and that we do not want to begrudge our Lord God the one day, the seventh, Sabbath, or rest day, alongside of a few other festivals." His conclusion is that since "the house of prayer and day of prayer are made into a house for selling and a day for selling among us evangelicals today" in such a crass manner, better conditions prevail in this point even among the papists.[379]

The church orders repeatedly spoke of how people were coarse, immoderate, immoral, and especially given to unrestrained gluttony. Archbishop Sigismund of Magdeburg spoke out against this with the most forceful tones. On the basis of the impressions his visitors had gained, he published his not very complimentary mandate concerning church discipline and included that it had reached his ears that his subjects "now and then fell into a coarse, filthy, wild, and ill-mannered life such that love, both toward God and the neighbor, had

---

[376] Herbert Koch, "Die Kirchenvisitation des Jahres 1582," *Zeitschrift des Vereins für Thüringische Geschichte und Altertumskunde* 40 (1936), 41–66; Delius.
[377] A region in Bayreuth and Bohemia surrounding the Eger River. – KGW
[378] Götz, *Wirren*, 36, 73.
[379] Sehling 2:357.

been totally extinguished in many, also [that they] spend their lives in open sin without any shame, like wild animals, without any fear of God, especially in villages." Of the common events for which he established draconian punishments, the mere titles of the twenty paragraphs of this mandate furnished a distinct image; some of them read: "Concerning impious servants," "Concerning drinking before and during the sermon," "Concerning daily drinking and gambling," "Concerning quarreling and fighting," "Concerning obscene dancing," "Concerning harassing and reviling, and other offenses."[380] Delius reports about congruous conditions (public lewdness, etc.) according to the visitation acts and thereby confirms the mandate's statements.[381]

Given that such a populace was coarse enough to get drunk on Sundays and take swings at each other in bars,[382] it was no more astonishing that the respect for the sanctity of God's house, or even the cemetery, left something to be desired. The church orders addressed the last point more than occasionally and sometimes depicted the corresponding events meticulously and rigorously. The cemetery—by night a playground for adolescents for all sorts of mischief, by day grazed on by livestock, and before, during, and after the service on Sundays, a meeting point for the people to trade, sell brandy, and pass on the village gossip—was usually not fenced in back then, and was therefore prey to every abuse. It would be a legalization of such abuse if the local clergyman was conferred the privilege of using it agriculturally, which of course happened only in isolated cases.[383] As long as it was not enclosed, nothing could stop the mischief. Roads and paths cut across it and livestock ran around on it; in some cases it served as a "*Schulneccss*" or urinal for the children, as a garbage dump, and finally—in the Upper Palatinate and Mark Brandenburg, and certainly also elsewhere—as a place where people poured out their "filth" and where individual dignitaries occasionally kept their dung piles.[384] Since the mid-sixteenth century the authorities pressed for enclosing the cemeteries "with walls, board

---

[380] Mandate from May 30, 1562, Sehling 2:411ff.

[381] Delius, 89f.

[382] Sehling 2:413, Magdeburg 1562.

[383] See the text following note 345 above.

[384] Cf. for example Götz, *Wirren*, 63, 332; the 1573 consistorial order of Brandenburg; the 1572 Schulenburg church order, Sehling 3:115, 150.

fences or other good fences, also beams and doors." They made this
the responsibility of the local authorities, village mayors, council
members, etc., imposed punishments on violations, and ordered that
"traveling across it shall not be permitted, even in cities."[385] It has
been shown that for individual areas, complaints about cemeteries
ceased at the start of the seventeenth century.[386]

As cavalierly as people treated the cemeteries, so also the church
buildings; at least they moved about them rather freely. The Amberg
council was by no means alone when it decided in 1581 that it should
step in against the wicked custom of people going right through the
church during the sermon and Communion, even on Sundays, in order
to shorten their path, sometimes being loaded down with all kinds of
wares, and hired special employees to abolish this.[387] The 1612
Danzig church order, for example, established fines and a legal venue
for fights, bodily injuries, and lewdness within the large St. Mary
church. Among the numerous employees of this church, one in
particular, the beadle, had "to wait in the church every day with a
whip when children were on their way to or from school, to prevent
them from yelling, chasing, or running in the church or cemetery";
another, the manure transporter, had "to remove the dung from the
cemetery and around the church"; yet another[388] had "to keep the
church and cemetery clean of all filth" with a shovel and a broom,
and in addition he was given a special assignment: "He should use
water often to wash away the stench in the corners of the church."
The same order decreed that "whoever carries piglets, pigs, baskets of
fish, half or whole rumps of meat, or any other unusual loads through
the church before noon or otherwise during a sermon or Vespers,"

---

[385] See the previous note.

[386] For the Upper Palatinate: Götz, *Wirren*, 332; the reasoning for fencing in
cemeteries is very nice in the 1573 Brandenburg order: "and since the
cemeteries of deceased Christians, who have been saved by Christ and shall
be raised again on the Last Day, are homes for sleeping, the cemeteries
should always be kept clean and beautiful," Sehling 3:115.

[387] Ramge, 133.

[388] This was the dog-whipper (*Hundepeitscher*), so called because his duties
included driving dogs out of the church, although, among other things, he
was also to drive out misbehaving boys. Incidentally, the dog-whipper and
beadle (*Steckenknecht*) are both defined by the Latin word *virgarius* (rod-
bearer), but the order has an article for each in succession (Sehling 4:217). –
KGW

should count on his wares being confiscated. To enforce this regulation there were special watchmen, a kind of church police.[389] A special phenomenon, also aimed at in Danzig, appears to have been widespread at that time and not confined to only one land or confession: Here I am thinking of the custom of bringing dogs along into the service. Aside from Danzig, this can be shown for Thuringia, the Archbishopric of Trier, and southern France. In some places this was countered by introducing the office of a dog-whipper, who had to chase the animals out of the temple during the service.[390]

B. POPULAR CUSTOMS, SUPERSTITION, WITCHCRAFT

Everyone who is versed a little in the history of the late Middle Ages knows that superstition also flourished then alongside strong faith: an uncritical mania for miracles and a vigorous devotion to many forms of magic, fortune-telling, witchcraft, etc. According to all indications, these things were firmly and tenaciously rooted in the lives of people in that period, such that it was inconceivable to remove them with a hasty operation. Some superstitions were even reflected in the first printed missals. The evangelical and Catholic authorities of the sixteenth century indefatigably battled their various forms—speaking blessings (*Segensprechen*),[391] crystal-gazing, fortune-telling (*das "böten, wicken, warseggen"*), magical rites, symbolical acts, incantations, and anything else of the sort; on the whole, however, they achieved only few results. There was hardly a religion mandate,

---

[389] Sehling 4:201, 216f.; the regulation of their pay is also spoken of there.

[390] Sehling 4:217; the Henneberg Mandate of 1545, Sehling 2:285; Balthasar Fischer, "Ein Sonntagshochamt vor 400 Jahren," *Trierer Theologische Zeitschrift* 66 (1957) 176; Felix Platter's autobiography, ed. by Otto Fischer (*Thomas und Felix Platters und Theodor Agrippa d'Aubignés Lebensbeschreibungen.* München 1911), 236f.

[391] "*Segensprechen*: attempting to influence events by means of spells and blessings. . . . A *Segen* was a magic prayer, a *Segensprecher*, a speaker of 'blessings,' was a practitioner of verbal magic. Someone 'blessing' a cow to be fruitful or an axe to make short work, or asking to be 'blessed' in order to stay clear of trouble, was exerting a magic and—he believed—effective influence on the superior powers who granted such boons," p. 70f. in Gerald Strauss, "Staying Out of Trouble in the Sixteenth Century: A German Charm to Ward Off Evil," *Folklore Forum: A Communication for Students of Folklore* 14.2 (1981): 69–83. – KGW

visitation instruction, or larger church order that did not aim at abolishing witchcraft and superstitions by threatening punishment.

On the border between Christian faith and magical-superstitious notions lay many customs and practices celebrated on particular festivals or saints' feasts. Widespread was the St. John's Fire already mentioned before[392]; in the Upper Palatinate people took pieces of wood from it and carried them onto the fields in the hope that then the flax would grow as long as possible; when the fire was forbidden, people went elsewhere to get the brands and stick them in their fields.[393] In some places of the Upper Palatinate people bound their trees at Christmas, so that they would bear much fruit, and on Shrove-Tuesday they stuck birch branches in the manure, so that the livestock would rub against it.[394] On Walpurgis' Day in Pomerania, people hung mugwort and lettuce in the gate to ward off evil magic.[395]

Independently of the church festival times, but in connection with the natural seasons or with big events in a person's life, people also clung to certain conventions: Women who had just given birth had willow branches tied into their bed; after funerals people would expressly sound the bells because they imagined that the soul of the deceased sat upon the "church cross"—probably the church tower cross—until someone freed it by sounding the bells following the funeral.[396] In various places people hung bundles and crosses in the fruit trees, which was supposed to cause any thieves to "wither" and die after consuming the stolen fruit.[397] Since it is so well known that the belief in witches had struck deep roots in all social and educational strata, it is unnecessary to go into that here. How deep down it was even among elevated evangelical clergy can be illustrated with two small examples: A Lutheran visitation

---

[392] See the text following note 242 above.

[393] Götz, *Wirren*, 238, 349, 355.

[394] Götz, *Wirren*, 238; a further summary of customs and practices bordering on superstition is at 349f., notes 72–74; for a similar Lenten custom, also in Schleswig-Holstein, see Feddersen, 546.

[395] Hellmuth Heyden, *Kirchengeschichte Pommerns* vol. 1, p. 177 (2nd ed., Köln: R. Müller, 1957).

[396] An example opposed to this is in the 1540 report of the visitors to the rural district of Meissen: "The bells should be sounded for the dead so that the living also consider the hour and time of their death, better their lives, and be found as Christian people in faith." Sehling 1:565. – KGW

[397] Götz, *Wirren*, 82, 271, 298f.

commission of the Electoral Palatinate ordered the city council of Grafenwöhr to set up a watch on Walpurgis' Day on account of witches; the same commission summoned a woman in the city of Kastl to have her demonstrate before them how she supposedly could ride upon a fire-shovel.[398]

Notions that did not necessarily have to be superstitious, but could easily have become so, quite readily combined with churchly acts, formulas, and objects; to wit, comprehension of the effect of the sacraments was not free of magical-material notions. On the occasion of its explanation about Baptism, the 1531 Lübeck church order polemicized against the Catholic rites of consecration with baptismal water. It reproved the laity's taking the water by pots with permission of the priests (*Pfaffen*), "not for Baptism, but for abuse and sinful superstition," and said further that evidently "some cast spells with it."[399] From the great Saxon church order of Elector August which appeared in 1580, thus fifty years later, we know that the bell-ringer sold leftover Communion hosts, as well as baptismal water, and the people used them for "superstition." The 1581 Braunschweig-Grubenhagen church order expressed itself somewhat more clearly: When it ordered the sacristans to pour out the water immediately following the Baptism, or else lose their office and be punished severely, it wanted to prevent them from passing it on or selling it "to

---

[398] Götz, *Wirren*, 79f. The latest to appear on the phenomenon of belief in witches: Hugo Zwetsloot, *Friedrich Spee und die Hexenprozesse* (Trier: Paulinus-Verlag, 1954). [Grafenwöhr and Kastl are in the Upper Palatinate. Numerous books have been published more recently dealing with the topics of witchcraft and witch hunting and Europe. See, for example, Brian P. Levack. *The Witch-Hunt in Early Modern Europe*, 3rd ed. (Harlow; New York: Pearson Longman, 2006) and Robin Briggs, *Witches and Neighbours: The Social and Cultural Context of European Witchcraft*, 2nd ed. (Wiley-Blackwell, 2008). For studies more particular to Germany, see H. C. Erik Midelfort, *Witch Hunting in Southwestern Germany, 1562–1684: The Social and Intellectual Foundations* (Stanford: Stanford University Press, 1972), Wolfgang Behringer, trans. by J. C. Grayson, David Lederer, *Witchcraft Persecutions in Bavaria: Popular Magic, Religious Zealotry and Reason of State in Early Modern Europe* (Cambridge; New York: Cambridge University Press, 2003), Alison Rowlands, *Witchcraft Narratives in Germany: Rothenburg 1561–1652* (Manchester: Manchester University Press, 2003), and Lyndal Roper, *Witch Craze: Terror and Fantasy in Baroque Germany* (New Haven; London: Yale University Press, 2006).]

[399] Sehling 5:354, original text in Low German.

sorcerous, superstitious people" who abused it for healing their sick livestock.[400] The visitation acts from the Upper Palatinate confirm this impression; people there used baptismal water in the stall for the livestock's health, to increase the productivity of fruit trees, to protect the cabbage field from worms and caterpillars, and also for pregnant girls (so that the whores would have children and thus their sin would be manifest).[401] The 1544/45 synodical instruction of Merseburg revealed something very remarkable: It prescribed that at Baptism only the element of water should be used, not "small beer,[402] malmsey, or milk, as has happened in some places."[403]

Aside from this Merseburg curiosity, the explanation of which is uncertain, the remaining reports awaken the impression that certain pre-Reformation notions of rites pertaining to the church year, the sacraments, or other churchly matters continued, here and there at any rate, and had long-lasting effects. If, however, they went on flourishing undeterred by the often severe prohibition orders, this presumably had to do principally with the local clergymen themselves sharing in the superstition of the people. This was almost altogether true for Schleswig-Holstein, according to Feddersen's research;[404] we shall supplement it here with some examples from central and southern Germany. When the daughter of a Franconian parson in the Margraviate of Ansbach—who on the whole was a good curate (*Seelsorger*), and incidentally also preached against superstitious acts on principle (indeed, an old parson's wife reproached him once on account of this)—was plagued by bouts of illness and no medical tactics succeeded, he himself decided to use a questionable remedy in this case; he took a "root"[405]—and behold!—his daughter's bouts subsided. In a territory with notoriously poor church attendance, in the rural district of the imperial city Ulm, only a single parson had a church that was packed full; however, he himself was an incantor and

---

[400] Sehling 1:426; 6/2:1049.

[401] Götz, *Wirren*, 96, 349; the cases mentioned lie partly around 1580, partly around 1615.

[402] *Kofent*, i.e. weak or inferior beer. – KGW

[403] Sehling 2:17.

[404] Feddersen, 541–547.

[405] *Wurz* could refer not only to a root, but also to an herb or plant in general, including petals, leaves, stems, blossoms, and fruit; cf. *DWB* "Wurz" 1. – KGW

treasure-seeker, healed toothaches in accordance with the waxing or waning of the moon, and knew all about the devil and exorcists. And finally, in the rural district of the city of Erfurt, a woman complained about her pastor because his efforts to heal her bedridden husband by means of incense as well as by bedaubing and conjuring with "blessings" had not brought any success—through which the whole affair then became known.[406]

C. IGNORANCE IN MATTERS OF FAITH

It is well known that the simple folk's knowledge of and familiarity with matters of faith was usually quite meager at the close of the Middle Ages. The church contented itself with a minimum and was satisfied if the people simply knew the Our Father, the Ten Commandments, and the Creed. These were precisely the items upon which the church orders laid value and about which the people were to be questioned again and again! This obligation, however, was by no means fulfilled everywhere, as we know from countless visitation reports, and this was because, among other reasons, the parsons themselves were not always the most well-versed. In light of what was said above about the background, avocational activities, and mediocre education of the clergy, this may not appear so inconceivable. The visitations in the region of Electoral Saxony, Merseburg, and Magdeburg offered material for this just as clear as those for the Upper Palatinate, the Electoral Palatinate, and the rural districts of Ulm and Nürnberg.[407] If one takes into account with this

---

[406] August Gabler, *Altfränkisches Dorf- und Pfarrhausleben 1559–1601* (Nürnberg: Die Egge, 1952), 20; passim there is substantial material on popular superstition; Julius Endriss, *Die Ulmer Kirchenvisitationen der Jahre 1557–1615* (Ulm: Hohn, 1937), 50f.; August Nebe, "Der Erfurter Landpastor im 17. Jahrhundert," *Zeitschrift des Vereins für Kirchengeschichte der Provinz Sachsen und des Freistaates Anhalt* 30 (1934), 110; relevant material is also in Heinz Dannenbauer, "Die Nürnberger Landgeistlichen bis zur zweiten Nürnberger Kirchenvisitation 1560/61," *Zeitschrift für bayerischen Kirchengeschichte* 2–9 (1927–1934) [2 (1927): 207–236; 3 (1928): 40–53, 65–79, 214–229; 4 (1929): 49–63, 107–122, 230–240; 6 (1931): 27–38, 109–116, 217–234; 7 (1932): 91–102, 221–242; 8 (1933): 215–230; 9 (1934): 40–51]; 25 (1956); healing of toothaches, for example, in the same article, p. 127 of vol. 25 (1956).
[407] Cf. Endriss and Dannenbauer in the previous note [see also Philip J. Broadhead, "Public Worship, Liturgy and the Introduction of the Lutheran

that the pastors usually did not bring much [knowledge] with them, did not always exactly continue studying in office, often pursued other means of breadwinning, read their sermons from the Postils, occasionally cancelled catechesis[408] or could not teach it because domestic servants stayed away from the (in principle mandatory) instruction and parents did not send their children,[409] or because landowners sat with their servants Sunday afternoons in taverns with beer,[410] then it simply could not be expected that the religious education would visibly improve in comparison with the Middle Ages. Thus the population lacked a deeper understanding of the evangelical faith also because, as a rule, the congregations were more ignorant than the clergy, who themselves only commanded a little knowledge.[411] The 1540 Brandenburg church order, among others, included the formula for the manner in which a parson should speak with someone making confession; it recommended beginning by inquiring after the person's knowledge of the Ten Commandments and presupposed that the answer would be: "Dear sir, unfortunately I cannot," and built the confessional dialog upon this foundation.[412] The historian of the Ulm church visitation, Julius Endriss, reported that shortly after 1600, i.e. about seventy years after the introduction of the Reformation, the existence of an abysmal ignorance among the populace of this imperial city's rural district had been confirmed and that, despite decades of (theoretical) catechism sermons, neither the old nor the young could properly recite the Lord's Prayer, but

---

Reformation in the Territorial Lands of Nuremberg," *English Historical Review* 120.486 (2005): 277–302]; Götz, *Bewegung*, Friedrich Hermann Otto Danneil, *Protokolle der ersten lutherischen General-Kirchen-Visitation im Erzstifte Magdeburg anno 1562–64* (Magdeburg: Selbstverlag des Herausgebers, 1864); Walter Friedensburg, *Protokolle der Kirchenvisitation im Stift Merseburg von 1562 und 1578* (Magdeburg: Selbstverlag der Historischen Kommission, 1931); Wilhelm Schmidt, "Die Kirchen- und Schulvisitation im sächsischen Kurkreise vom Jahre 1555," *Schriften des Vereins für Reformationsgeschichte* 90 and 92 (1906, "Erstes Heft: Die kirchlichen und sittlichen Zustände" and "Zweites Heft: Die wirtschaftlichen Verhältnisse"), passim in all.
[408] Götz, *Bewegung*, 152. [See note 357 above.]
[409] Götz, *Wirren*, 74, cf. also 298.
[410] Plantiko, 128f.
[411] Delius, 81, 89. Also for Prussia cf. the 1543 church order, Sehling 4:60f.
[412] Sehling 3:62.

miserably mangled, murdered, and martyrized it.[413] That which the historian of the evangelical church in Thuringia, Rudolf Herrmann, reports from the first half of the seventeenth century went in the same direction, although here the negative effects of the Thirty Years' War need to be taken into consideration when evaluating this. To illustrate the prevailing ignorance in matters of faith, Herrmann shares some of the recorded statements of congregation members in answer to the inquiries of the 1641 Gotha visitation. For example, to the question: "What does God promise to those who keep His commandments?" some answered: "Temporal death and eternal damnation"! Or to the question: "What shall we do if we have sinned against God?" some knew nothing better to answer than: "We should heartily thank Him for this."[414]

That may suffice for examples. Seen on the whole, they signal a tradition from the shadows of ecclesial life and also show in this point a connection between late medieval Catholicism and early modern Protestantism. Of course it is good constantly to remind oneself here that the responsible authorities relentlessly endeavored to counter the abuses that had been identified and put things in order—just as the Catholic authorities did after the Reformation, incidentally, though often not beginning until a little later. Beyond the fact of these efforts, what kind of transformation or improvement occurred is a separate question. On a broader basis this can probably be answered only by means of a penetrating study of the visitation records.

The preliminary overall impression left by the Lutheran church orders is surely one of a great wealth of traditions in ecclesial and worship practice, thus of a wealth of traditions precisely on that side of ecclesial life which was mostly devoted to the common man. While evangelical theology had long since gone its own way, polity, liturgy, and terminology continued moving down the same old paths for a long time. Certainly the emphasis on the sermon, the heavy use of the German language, the abbreviation of the Mass, and the removal of consecrations using water, salt, and herbs brought far-reaching renewal. In the face of this, however, the endurance of the

---

[413] Endriss, see notes 401 and 406 above; for other examples of ignorance of the Lord's Prayer, cf. Delius, 89 (pertaining to the Barnstedt parish in the subdistrict (*Amt*) of Querfurt).
[414] Rudolf Herrmann, *Thüringische Kirchengeschichte* vol. 2, p. 210f. (Weimar: Hermann Böhlaus Nachfolger, 1947).

old did in fact remain strong and impressive. On the liturgical front, where ecclesial events took place, not much changed on the whole; conditions of law and polity at a lower level likewise remained almost the same. And if, in view of the widespread lack of education among the spiritual estate before and right after the Reformation, one may deduce a comparable lack of theological education among the simple laypeople—for which there are in fact sundry indications—it is probably permissible to express as a justified assumption that these simple laypeople, especially of the rural congregations, perhaps did not altogether consciously grasp the reformational change which is so thoroughly present for us moderns as a division of faith and of the church. This is so first, because they did not understand much about theology, and second, because they continued to attend the same parish or out-parish church, pay the same fees, celebrate the same festivals, and were at most astonished when admonished more severely by their pastor and when the authorities took a stronger line with them—which, incidentally, likewise astonished the Catholic laity since the Tridentine reforms.

CONCLUSION

Throughout this perusal of the Lutheran church orders we have encountered traditions from the pre-Reformation, Catholic period in various levels of ecclesial life. These were met in the realm of liturgy and the administration of sacraments, to a lesser extent also in the conception of the sacraments; to a greater extent in the religious attitude in general, especially where this was expressed in customs and usages. Then we encountered older traditions in the area of law and polity, as well as economic conditions closely linked to these. Finally we saw that the abuses so greatly deplored at the close of the Middle Ages had a tenacious life of their own and by no means disappeared swiftly with the Reformation. On the contrary, they lived on in Protestantism and also caused trouble for the Lutheran authorities. For the time being, these things remain to be evaluated and historically interpreted; it is not possible to approach doing so until the proportions have been ascertained on the solid foundation of broadly conducted individual studies with more certainty than was possible with this more exploratory overview. The work in hand understands itself only as a first attempt in this direction. The author was incited to it by the question regarding the process of confessional formation, which has occupied him for a long time.

For all that, it may not be too soon to pursue some of the questions which were already asked in the early stages of our occupation with the material and which may perhaps offer a starting point for further observation and evaluation of it. Two of these I single out: the phenomenon of Lutheranism's conservative stance and the specific testimonial value of the church orders for historical knowledge.

The ecclesiastically conservative behavior of Lutheranism may be traced to various causes, not least of all from Luther's view that one may retain from the old churchdom whatever was not of downright unevangelical content, at least in certain situations.[415] This attitude

---

[415] For example, the elevation in the Lutheran Mass, *WA* 19:99 [cf. *LW* 53:82, The German Mass and Order of Service (1526)] abrogated by

benefited especially the ceremonies, the liturgy, and religious usages in the broader sense. One may suppose here that, precisely because Luther was not narrow-minded in the things he regarded as adiaphora, the law of custom and the power of what was handed down prevailed to a certain degree in liturgy, usages, and other specialized areas. If it was indeed understandable that much of what had taken root and found form in the space of the church prior to the Reformation remained beyond the Reformation, this was by no means self-evident. The counterexample of the fanatics and Calvinism teaches this.

Fidelity to tradition was not thoroughly uniform. Rather, some churchmen and princely personages appeared to be bound to tradition less, others more—as Georg of Anhalt and Joachim II of Brandenburg, as well as numerous cathedral and collegiate chapters. Likewise, individual cities and countrysides especially liked persisting in old forms and establishments of the church; among these were, for example, east-central Germany (Brandenburg, the Old and New Mark, the Lusatias [Upper and Lower], Silesia, chapter and diocesan lands of the middle-Elbian region), as well as Lower Saxony, West Prussia, and the Upper Palatinate.

If Luther's attitude—unfavorable to radicalism and partially benevolent to tradition—especially benefited the liturgy or "ceremonies," some other circumstances also contributed essentially to the propensity for liturgical tradition. In the course of the transformation at the beginning of the Reformation, vast freedoms came to be demanded and exercised. Around the time of the Peasants' War, however, when alongside of the Lutheran movement all sorts of fanatic, Anabaptist, and spiritualistic movements arose, which were quite apparently carried by the tendency to push forward the Reformation much farther than Luther had ever envisioned, Luther himself and likewise the authorities of evangelical territories and cities stepped hard on the brakes. Also, since the secondary movements of fanatics reformed the service very freely, liberally, and radically, the territorial churches forming at that time vigorously emphasized in opposition to this the necessity of a service with a rigid order and conservative forms. Probably the greatest reason for the

---

Bugenhagen in 1542 with Luther's consent; cf. elucidations on the German Mass by Otto Dietz and Georg Merz in the Munich edition of Luther's works, *Ausgewählte Werke* 3rd ed. [ed. by Hans Heinrich Borcherdt, München: Christian Kaiser, 1950] 3:418.

inner-evangelical conflict that was appearing lay in the different conception of the sacraments, Scripture, and the church. Yet for internal reasons the variation in conception also necessarily had a retroactive effect on worship forms, particularly on the rites for administering the sacraments. Thus the fanatic movements indirectly helped to strengthen the conservative line of the Lutheran liturgy. Calvinism had a similar indirect effect primarily in the latter half of the century; first, however, a direct impulse proceeded in this direction, even if the effect was different, from the Interim at about the middle of the century (1548). Graff pointed out that the Interim, which, as is known, demanded the reintroduction of candles, surplices, use of Latin for certain parts of the service, and more of the like, caused some cities in southern Germany to accept a richer book of ceremonies, while in contrast some cities and lands in the Rhine-Westphalia region abrogated ceremonies (which they had maintained until that time) out of disgust for the Interim and in order to demonstrate that they wanted to have nothing to do with it.[416] According to evidence from the Lutheran church orders, about the same applied for southern as for central and eastern Germany: In various places there, the Interim induced the return to a richer liturgy, which then often remained for a long time.

When the political powers also began to take special interest in the liturgy since the middle of the sixteenth century, consistently carried along by the idea that not only confessional unity, but also ceremonial uniformity within territorial borders was desirable and therefore to be striven for, and as they established their ecclesiastical and secular bureaucracy in order to accomplish these intentions, the natural result was that a certain legality came to the worship forms— thus precisely that which Luther had wanted to avoid, but which could not be avoided in the long run because, as Luther had to admit already in 1526, "the multiplicity that had grown from this deregulation," had degenerated "into offensive confusion."[417] This development toward solidifying the service in a half-Catholic world of forms gained further impetus with the rise of Calvinism in the latter half of the century. Calvin himself was not a friend of the Lutheran ceremonies, but recommended that his brothers in faith

---

[416] Graff 1:17.
[417] Schmidt, 57. [Schmidt refers to Luther's preface to "The German Mass and Order of Service," cf. *LW* 53:61.]

tolerate them if they found themselves to be a small minority in Lutheran environs in Germany—insofar as certain Reformed doctrinal convictions would not thereby be violated.[418] Where Calvinism dominated, on the other hand, there was no more talk of such toleration; within Germany this applied to Nassau and numerous Reformed counties in western Germany, for the communities on the Lower Rhine, and for the Electoral and Upper Palatinate. Crucifixes and altars, surplice and houseling cloth, exorcism and singing in Latin, private confession and absolution, the spiritual office's power of the keys, consecration of bread and wine, and emergency Baptism were regarded by the Reformed as papistic and idolatrous; and because the Lutherans held fast to them, the Reformed considered them in this point as half-Catholics. Olevian, the Calvinistic reformer of the Electoral Palatinate, expressed himself with bitter earnest in a sermon in Amberg before a Lutheran congregation concerning the Lutheran manner of receiving the Lord's Supper: "You go to the Sacrament, raise your hands, kneel down, and allow a little cloth to be held under you; that is an idolatry to which eternal damnation belongs." On the same occasion he designated the consecration in the Lutheran Mass as "idolatry," which had never "been practiced under the sun to such an extent as in Amberg and in the papacy."[419] Lutheran parsons who used the surplice had to endure being called gross papists. The Reformed visitors explicitly called the hosts [altar bread] in the Supper, against which they had a special battle, papistic Mass-hosts, and, in order to ruin the Lutheran congregations' taste for them, told them that these hosts were "entirely unhealthy" and that people would get "jaundice, dropsy, swollen stomachs, and fevers from them."[420] Against such massive allegations universally levied from the Calvinistic side,[421] the Lutherans reacted with a stronger recourse to ceremonies, among other things. Indeed, ceremonies

---

[418] Cf. Ernst Walter Zeeden, "Calvins Verhalten zum Luthertum," in *Festschrift Karl Eder zum siebzigsten Geburtstag*, ed. by Helmut J. Mezler-Andelberg (Innsbruck: Wagner, 1959).
[419] Ramge 115f.
[420] Götz, *Wirren*, 245, 268f., 291, 310, 334; Götz, *Einführung*, 97, 109, 127, 132f., 137f.
[421] Cf. also the 1598 advisory opinion of the Berlin theologians, Müller, 528f.: our adversaries, "who are in the habit of calling such ceremonies monuments of papistic idolatry. . . . "

became the very means for them to ward off (or unmask) Calvinism. It did not represent a merely personal conviction when, near the end of his life, Elector Joachim II of Brandenburg said in the preface to a German breviary and missal for the Berlin cathedral (1568) that the confessional confusion in the evangelical churches arose not least of all because "in many places Christian hymns and readings have been completely abolished."[422] At the close of the sixteenth century some church orders prescribed careful observation of the liturgical ceremonies in order, as it says, for example, in an ordinance for Lower Lusatia (1592), "to stop the harmful, abhorrent, misleading Calvinistic sect in this Margraviate of Lower Lusatia in the country as well as in the cities."[423] Since in fact liturgical traditions, vestments, church vessels, etc., were immediately removed wherever Calvinism infiltrated or Reformed ideas even gained influence in the church's polity, the reaction which it caused in Lutheran areas was a conscious propensity for ceremonies. Henceforth, therefore, the celebration of an emphatically liturgical service was among the visible signs by which the Lutheran character of confession was demonstrated outwardly.

---

[422] Müller, 340. Until the middle of the nineties his daughter Elisabeth Magdalena, in her capacity as chief cathedral inspector (*oberste Dominspektorin*), resolutely held to the conservative worship forms there because she hoped that, "as long as such ceremonies would remain in Mark Brandenburg, . . . the Calvinistic impertinence would also cease in the public church office [Mass]." Müller, 340.

[423] Sehling 3:363; more from the text of this church order [of Landvogt Jaroslav Kolovrat]: "Since, however, the church ceremonies have been instituted for the sake of adornment and good order . . . [and], as outward marks, distinguish the true church of God from the false, it is not without good reason that we are moved to return the Christian ceremonies (which have fallen into disuse to strengthen the Calvinistic error and disdain religion and hinder God's honor) to a proper state . . . "; cf. also the 1568 Prussian church order, Sehling 4:73: "Therefore [we] also could not side with the grievous Calvinists and fanatics, who imagine that one cannot be evangelical if one does not destroy all paintings, tear down all pictures, abolish all ceremonies, and let everything fall into confusion grossly, immodestly, without any discipline or order, like irrational beasts. Such may please them as it will; we know that nothing happens thereby which pleases God, who is not a God of disorder, 1 Cor. 14, much less which edifies and improves the church."

With Luther being untroubled by using ancient church forms (as long as they appeared evangelically usable to him), with the reaction to the fanatics and Calvinism, and with the partial influence of the Interim, surely not all, but definitely several important causes have been identified which explain the conservative behavior of Lutheranism in liturgical matters. Of course there are many things in addition to this. Luther, for example, as well as many fellow reformers and helpers of the Reformation following his example had quite a strong pastoral-pedagogical regard for the weak, for whose sake some things were left as before. Occasionally, though with varying effects, a certain respect for the neighboring political territory also played in. The regard for subjects of another confession in the nearby environs could prompt the removal as well as further encouragement or tolerance of older churchly practices. In Coburg, the visitors of 1554/55 had the sounding of the bells at *Salve* time discontinued "for the sake of foreign and neighboring people" with the argument: "so that people will not regard us" (in the Franconian vicinity?) "as papistic."[424] In contrast, people in Fraustadt celebrated Corpus Christi in view of their Catholic neighbors—true, not with a procession, but at least with a sermon about the Sacrament of the Altar;[425] and in the Upper Palatine subdistrict (*Amt*) of Cham, even the otherwise so reviled "*idola*" [images, idols] were allowed to stand—on account of the spatial proximity to Catholic Bavaria.[426]

So much for suggestions to explain the ecclesiastically conservative behavior of Lutheranism in central, northern, and eastern Germany. Now on to the second and last point, a remark about the church orders as sources of our historical knowledge. As a qualification we will have to say in advance that the church orders, insofar as they deal with laws and ordinances that demanded and determined what should be done and what not, do not deliver more than other laws: They permit us to take cognizance of what the governing entity desired, permitted, allowed, or forbade. The extent to which these things were implemented or only remained on paper,

---

[424] Sehling 1:544. [See the text at note 292 above.]
[425] Sehling 4:293f.: "Corpus Christi Day ... should be kept for the neighbor's sake, to avoid [giving] offense." [This is in an admonition to the guild of tradesmen in Fraustadt by Andreas Knoblauch, which was ratified in 1564.]
[426] Götz, *Wirren*, 272.

however, evades our knowledge, unless parallel sources are available to us, and constitutes a certain limitation of the church orders for our understanding. Nevertheless, even these mere guidelines, demands, and prohibitions are not totally devoid of importance; under circumstances it can indeed be valuable that, with their help, we can learn what the political powers wanted and aimed at, and the tendencies by which they were carried. Thus the church orders yield many things, for example, for understanding the direction in which the development of the territorial state of the sixteenth century moved. Yet by no means do these orders direct themselves solely towards a desirable target state. Rather, they also continuously address the state at the time of their composition, with which they are concerned and upon which they want to act. They target the existing conditions by either describing them or, more frequently, deploring them, and by demanding that some things found in practice be abolished or some things not found in practice be observed from that time on. For example, when an order stipulates how much money should be paid out to the dog-whippers in the church and how severe a punishment should be meted out to dog owners who, as it says in a mandate from the count of Henneberg,[427] do not chain up their "dogs and curs in their homes when the service is customarily held in the churches with Mass, preaching, and other [things]," but instead let them run into the churches, where they "restively tumble together, as has happened up to now, with barking and yelping"—the respective penal regulation would be somewhat idealistic if it did not aim at a particular habit, or rather, bad habit. Whoever reads closely and prudently will be able to find out a lot of factual information from the church orders. In this respect, they are a multifaceted source. Quite a lot is hidden within them, not only for a history of religious customs and ecclesiastical establishments, but also for the cultural and social history of the sixteenth century, especially for a social history of the evangelical pastoral estate (*Pfarrstand*), for a history of the political authorities' consciousness of religious offices, and for a history of evangelical ecclesiastical and matrimonial law. Furthermore, through comparative analysis of the orders in a territorial district in chronological order, one can ascertain more or less what was preserved and gradually became the base stock of ecclesial and religious life, and what was not preserved and was eliminated. All of

---

[427] Sehling 2:284f.

this can be examined more closely, of course, where the sources concerning implementation of church organization have been preserved, thus visitation acts and records; however, they are not always readily available to us, let alone extant; even in this case, we must attempt to make a beginning with the church orders. Finally, let it be noted that these orders were interspersed with sections of an instructive and reflective character. Flowing beneath it all, of course, there is a lot of flowery speech with then-current turns of phrase. For one thing, however, many an original phrase and idea, and many a deep thought also stand between the expressions; for another thing, even stereotypes and supra-individual behavior[428] are most informative for an historical epoch's horizon, pathos, way of thinking, and awareness of time and history.

Finally, I would like to think it will be especially worthwhile at some point to view the Lutheran church orders of the sixteenth century in comparison with the Reformed orders and the Tridentine reform decretals (and the religion mandates and implementation laws in the Catholic dioceses and principalities that correspond to them) and to investigate their differences and similarities on a broad base. Beyond the sphere of the consolidation of the church's polity, dogma, and the liturgy, such a comparative investigation will help—that is the hope, anyway—to unlock with more certainty the phenomena concerning contemporary history which are of particular interest to the general historian. Here I am thinking primarily of the confessionalization phenomenon characteristic of the early modern era in connection with the cultural, social, and political developments in particular, and in general with the ways of living and ways of thinking in the age of the Reformation, Counter-Reformation, and inner-Catholic reform.

This study of the history of the development of confessional churchdom is, however, as everyone knows, more than just a study of an historically bound phenomenon. For the things that developed at that time in history are, to put it mildly, problematic and painful matters in the category of dogma and church (*sub specie dogmatis et ecclesiae*)—matters and problems which, because they are acute to this day, also make the investigation of their historical origins in the

---

[428] [*das*] *Überindividuelle*—the concept is that of innate and learned behavior as a result of the time and place in which someone lives. – KGW

age of schism relevant (in an entirely unsensationalist sense) up to the present day.

Indexes

I. Index of Persons, Places, and Territories

Leuchtenberg, 68

Liegnitz, 21, 22, 85

Lippe, 44

Livonia, xii

Loccum, 51

Löscher, Valentin Ernst, 58, 61

Lübeck, 35, 36, 51, 56, 78, 90, 99, 107

Lucenius, Albert, 50

Lüneburg, 15, 17, 19, 20, 35, 49, 51

Lusatia, 32, 61

Lusatia, Lower, 32, 56, 114, 117

Lusatia, Upper, 54, 61, 114

Luther, Martin, ix, 1, 2, 3, 9, 10, 11, 14, 15, 16, 18, 19, 21, 23, 24, 26, 27, 34, 36, 37, 42, 43, 49, 50, 54, 60, 64, 73, 74, 79, 80, 84, 96, 97, 113, 114, 115, 118

Magdeburg, 9, 10, 32, 34, 42, 48, 89, 90, 100, 102, 103, 109, 110

Mainz, xviii, 17

Mansfeld, 21, 74, 80, 83, 85

Mark, County of, 56, 58

Mark, Electoral, 17, 37, 56, See Brandenburg

Mark, New, xvii, 24, 114

Mark, Old, xvii, 17, 24, 80, 114

Mary, Virgin, 16, 60, 70, 73, See feasts

Mazovia, 69

Mecklenburg, 15, 22, 23, 32, 38, 54, 55, 67, 78, 81, 82, 83, 84, 88, 89, 97

Meissen, 44, 106

Melanchthon, Philipp, xv, xvi, 2, 27, 34, 35, 40, 41, 42, 49, 80, 84

Menius, Julius, 13

Merseburg, 28, 108, 109, 110

Michael monastery (in Lüneburg), 51

Michael, St., 55, See feasts

Minden, xvii, 22, 52, 55

Moritz, Elector of Saxony, xix, 35, 61

Musculus, Andreas, 25

Musculus, Wolfgang, 11, 12, 14

Nabburg, 68

Nassau, 116

Neumarkt, 37, 38

Nicolas, Bishop of Verdun, 21

Nittenau, 29

Nordhausen, 61, 62

Nördlingen, 22

Northeim, 15, 56

Nürnberg, xvii, 9, 18, 20, 27, 33, 55, 60, 90, 109, 110

Oldenburg in Holstein, 83

Olevian, Kaspar, 43, 116

Osnabrück, xvii, 50, 51, 53

Osterode in East Prussia, 70, 90

Ostrorog, 61

II. INDEX OF SUBJECTS

cross, church tower, 106

cross, sign of the, 36, 37, 38, 39, 46

crucifix, 37, 38, 116, *See* cross

crystal-gazing, 105

cultic, 58

cultural history, 29, 119

cultural standing, 93

cur, 119

curate, xii, xiii, 82, 108

cursing, 96

custom(s), xxv, 7, 8, 17, 21, 23, 28, 34, 36, 37, 44, 47, 48, 52, 55, 58, 62, 63, 64, 65, 68, 69, 70, 74, 86, 87, 88, 94, 96, 104, 105, 106, 113, 114, 119

customary, xiii, 14, 35, 38, 83, 86, 88, 89, 119

daily office prayers, 17

daily offices, xiv, *See* choir offices

dancing, 98, 100, 103

datio salis, 42, 43

deacon, xiii, 12, 13, 14, 19

dean, -ery, xvii, 30, 77

declaration, 97

decree, xiv, 18, 36, 61, 62, 73, 80, 85, 89

decretals, 84, 85, 120

degeneration, 94, 100

delegation, 45

department, 39

desecration, 4, 100, 102

devil, 43, 62, 82, 109

devil's work, 38

devotion, -al, xxv, 9, 28, 36, 60, 63, 65, 66, 105

didactic, 34

dignitaries, 38, 103

diocesan estate, 89

diocesan lands, 114

diocese, 18, 48, 120

disciplinary authority, 81, 82

disease, 58, 68

distribution (of the Sacrament), 23, 25, 28, 37, 40

distribution formula, 23

district, xv, 32, 48

divine right, 81

divine service, xxv, 5, 50, 53, 75

divorce, 78

doctor (physician), 44, 61

doctrinal authority, 3

doctrinal ordinance, 2

doctrinal quarrels, 24

dog, 89, 105, 119

dogma, dogmatic, 4, 40, 78, 120

dog-whipper, 105, 119

donkey (wooden), 64

door bars, 101

dove, 64

drinking, 62, 98, 99, 103

dropsy, 116

drunkenness, 4, 90, 97, 98

dung, 104

money (for attendance), 52

monstrance, 24, 33

moon, 109

moral, 4, 93, 94

moral discipline, 3

moral mandate, 4

mother, 44, 45

Mount of Olives, 9, 20

mugwort, 106

municipal promulgation, 100

mystery, 26

New Testament, 9, 35, 41

New Year, 53

nobility, xvii, xviii, 86, 87

notarial, 90

nourishment, 61, 90

nuptial mass, 47

occasional fees, xiii, 39, 91

offense, xvi, 4, 28, 34, 36, 37, 43, 57, 80, 83, 100, 103, 118

offering, 15, 45, 68, 69, 83, 86

offering box, xiii, 69

offertory, 14, 21

Office (Mass), 10, 12, 27, 117

Office of the Keys, xvi, 49, 54, 116, *See* binding key

old covenant, 41

Old Testament, 9, 35, 59

ordaining minister, 48

ordinance, 2, 3, 4, 64, 70, 78, 91, 94, 117, 118

ordination, 40, 41, 42, 48, 53, 85

Ordo Missae, 8

organ, -ist, xiv, 12, 13

ornament, 32

orthodoxy, 25, 58

ostension, 24, 25, 63

Our Father, 16, 20, 99, 109

out-parish, xiii, 77, 112

oven, 88

oxen, 88

papacy, 1, 7, 11, 31, 44, 54, 61, 70, 71, 116

papism, papistic, 7, 11, 12, 13, 23, 29, 42, 54, 58, 70, 79, 80, 116, 118

parents, 79, 110

parish, x, xii, xiii, xv, 11, 32, 77, 78, 83, 87, 91, 94, 95, 102, 111, 112

parish library, 18, 96

parishioners, x, xiii, 24

parity, 56

parson, xii, xv, xvi, 4, 19, 29, 30, 32, 35, 37, 38, 44, 45, 49, 63, 69, 72, 77, 80, 81, 83, 85, 86, 87, 88, 89, 90, 91, 94, 95, 96, 97, 98, 100, 108, 109, 110, 116, *See* clergy *and* curate

parsonage, xiii, 86

Passion Week, 9, 63, 64

Passiontide, 8, 58, 59

pastor, x, xi, xii, xiii, xiv, xvi, 38, 71, 72, 74, 75, 79, 82, 87, 88, 89, 90, 91, 94, 95, 97, 98, 99, 109, 110, 112, *See* parson

preface, 14, 16, 20, 21, 22, 26

preparatory prayers, 15

pre-Reformation, xxv, 18, 21, 25, 26, 27, 31, 33, 36, 46, 50, 56, 59, 64, 70, 86, 93, 108, 112, 113, 114

presentation, right of, 77, 95

price raising, 61

priest, -ly, xii, 7, 13, 15, 19, 25, 26, 27, 28, 30, 34, 39, 41, 47, 48, 49, 71, 79, 87, 95, 107

prince, -ly, xiii, xv, xviii, 2, 3, 24, 28, 44, 51, 67, 68, 78, 79, 83, 89, 99, 114

principality, xviii, 63, 120

private Mass, 26, 27

privilegium fori, 7, 85

procession, 8, 17, 31, 33, 39, 50, 51, 52, 56, 63, 64, 65, 66, 118

procession poles, 31, 33

Professio fidei Tridentinae, 52

prohibition, 61, 62, 63, 67, 82, 97, 108, 119

promise, 13, 42, 47, 49, 59, 111

Protestant, -ism, x, xvii, xxv, 1, 3, 4, 5, 24, 27, 40, 52, 57, 63, 69, 78, 83, 91, 111, 113

provost, xvii, 65

psalm, 9, 10, 11, 14, 17, 19, 20, 34, 36, 51

pulpit, 82, 96

punishment, 4, 67, 79, 81, 82, 84, 98, 101, 103, 104, 119,

See ecclesiastical punishment, secular punishment

punishment threat, 86, 106

punitive measure, 100

purgatory, 50

Quadragesima, 61, 62

quarterly fee, 59

radicalism, 114

reading, 9, 12, 16, 19, 20, 26, 28, 37, 43, 50, 54, 59, 97, 117

realism, realistic, 25, 28, 30

recitation, 20, 23

records, xvi

reform, ix, xiii, 1, 2, 18, 23, 35, 112, 114, 120

Reformation, ix, x, xiii, xvi, xvii, xviii, xxv, 1, 3, 4, 5, 8, 11, 14, 15, 18, 19, 22, 23, 24, 30, 33, 35, 37, 40, 47, 48, 49, 54, 57, 62, 66, 67, 72, 75, 78, 86, 87, 88, 89, 93, 94, 99, 110, 111, 112, 113, 114, 118, 120

Reformed, xxv, 3, 11, 12, 31, 38, 44, 58, 95, 116, 117, 120

reformer, reformational, 30, 42, 50, 51, 84, 112, 116, 118

regent, xv, 24, 62

region, ix, xii, xiii, xvii, xix, 17, 36, 65, 67, 88, 101, 102, 109, 114, 115

Peer Reviewed

Concordia Publishing House

Similar to the peer review or "refereed" process used to publish professional and academic journals, the Peer Review process is designed to enable authors to publish book manuscripts through Concordia Publishing House. The Peer Review process is well-suited for smaller projects and textbook publication.

We aim to provide quality resources for congregations, church workers, seminaries, universities, and colleges. Our books are faithful to the Holy Scriptures and the Lutheran Confessions, promoting the rich theological heritage of the historic, creedal Church. Concordia Publishing House (CPH) is the publishing arm of The Lutheran Church—Missouri Synod. We develop, produce, and distribute (1) resources that support pastoral and congregational ministry, and (2) scholarly and professional books in exegetical, historical, dogmatic, and practical theology.

For more information, visit:
www.cph.org/PeerReview.

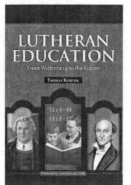

Lutheran Education: From Wittenberg to the Future

Thomas Korcok

"Dr. Korcok's book comes at the perfect time. . . . This book shows that Lutherans have a rich educational heritage, one that lives today and that holds great promise for the future."
—From the Foreword by Dr. Gene Edward Veith, Provost and Professor of Literature, Patrick Henry College

Thomas Korcok explores the historical Lutheran model of education in view of theological truths and how that model might be used today. The book includes: the influences that push educators either to the Word as objective truth or away from the Word toward secular standards of truth; a definition of an Evangelical liberal arts approach, its flexibility, and how it fits into classrooms today; and extensive references to educational, historical, and theological literature.

(P) 328 pages. Paperback.

53-1189LBR   **978-0-7586-2834-3**

The Real Luther: A Friar at Erfurt and Wittenberg

Franz Posset

"Students and researchers should read this book as a model for how to do Reformation History."
—Dr. Markus Wriedt, Goethe University Frankfurt/Main and Marquette University

Roman Catholic Scholar, Franz Posset, carefully explores the history of Luther's development in the crucial years of 1501–17 before Luther's views were disputed. Setting aside legends and accusations, Posset clearly presents the facts about Luther as a late medieval friar in an age of reform.

The Real Luther includes: illustrations from Luther's career; a complete, new translation of Philip Melanchthon's memoirs of Luther's life based on actual discussions with Luther; a fresh chronology of Luther's life from 1501–17, based on the latest research; and extensive references to both primary and secondary literature for Luther studies. (P) 224 pages. Paperback.

53-1180LBR   **978-0-7586-2685-1**

---

www.cph.org • 1-800-325-3040

Concordia
Publishing House

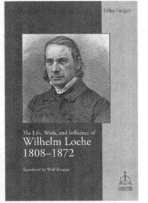

The Life, Work, and Influence of

Wilhelm Loehe 1808 – 1872

Erika Geiger; translated by Wolf Knappe

"This first, full-length biography of a key player in Lutheran history is accessible to lay audiences and appreciated by scholars."
—Prof. John T. Pless, Concordia Theological Seminary, Fort Wayne

The latest and best biography of a father of confessional Lutheranism in North America.

Loehe, who never visited the United States, sent missionaries, founded seminaries, established deaconess training, studied doctrine and liturgy, and fought with church officials. Geiger sets forth Loehe's life, and the divided opinions about him, in a compelling and authoritative narrative. (P) 296 pages. Paperback.

53-1176LBR   **978-0-7586-2666-0**

C. F. W. Walther: Churchman and Theologian

Various Authors

Called "the American Luther," Rev. Dr. C. F. W. Walther is celebrated as a founder of the log cabin college (1839) that became one of the ten largest seminaries in North America: Concordia Seminary, St. Louis. The educational emphasis and precedents Walther set made his theological heirs highly influential in American Christianity.

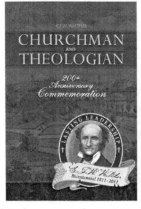

In 1847, when Walther helped to found The Lutheran Church—Missouri Synod, the church body included only 19 pastors, 30 congregations, and 4,099 baptized members. At the time of his death forty years later, the church body had grown to 931 pastors, 678 member congregations, 746 affiliated congregations, 544 preaching stations, and 459,376 baptized members.

C. F. W. Walther: Churchman and Theologian includes the winning essays from the 2011 Reformation Theology Research Award as well as an extensive Walther bibliography, providing the latest and best research on C. F. W. Walther in commemoration of the 200th anniversary of his birth. (P) 216 pages. Paperback.

53-1171LBR   **978-0-7586-2560-1**

---

www.cph.org • 1-800-325-3040   Concordia
                                                     Publishing House

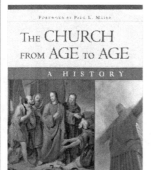

The Church from Age to Age

A History from Galilee to Global Christianity

General Editor Edward A. Engelbrecht

"An outstanding book! ... Combines all the elements that make for a great text."
—Dr. Robert Caldwell, Southwestern Baptist Theological Seminary

The Church from Age to Age examines key historic events from the time of the apostles through today. Informative and clearly written, readers of all ages will find the answers to the who, why, and how behind the current state of Christianity the world over. Maps, readings from primary sources, and an extensive bibliography, index, and timeline make this a complete one-volume resource for the classroom and for home.

Contributors include Robert G. Clouse, Karl H. Dannenfeldt, Edward A. Engelbrecht, Marianka S. Fousek, Walter Oetting, K. Detlev Schulz, Roy A. Suelflow, and Carl A. Volz. (P) 1048 pages. Paperback.

12-4370LBR   **978-0-7586-2646-2**

Friends of the Law: Luther's Use of the Law for the Christian Faith

Edward A. Engelbrecht

"For more than a century, each generation of scholars has produced a definitive study that redefines our understanding of Luther's signature teaching on the 'uses of the law'. Edward Engelbrecht's impressive new title is the definitive study for our generation." —Dr. John Witte, Jr., Emory University

Charges of forgery, heresy, legalism, and immorality turn on the question of whether Martin Luther taught a third use of the Law for the Christian life. For the past sixty years, well-meaning scholars believed they settled the question—with dire consequences.

Friends of the Law sets forth a completely new body of evidence that shows how little Luther's teaching was understood. This new book looks at the doctrine of the Law and invites a new consensus that could change the way Christians view the Reformation and even their daily walk with God. (P) 326 pages. Paperback.

12-4393LBR   **978-0-7586-3138-1**

www.cph.org • 1-800-325-3040   Concordia
                                                     Publishing House

BX 8067 .A1 Z4413 2012
Zeeden, Ernst Walter.
Faith and act

CPSIA information can be obtained at www.ICGtesting.com
Printed in the USA
LVOW090615240812

295728LV00003BA/2/P